The Single Woman in the Family of God

MARGARET BRITTON

The Single Woman
in the Family of God

EPWORTH PRESS

7162 0376 6

First published 1982
by Epworth Press
Room 195, 1 Central Buildings, Westminster, London SW1

Typeset by Gloucester Typesetting Services
and printed in Great Britain by
Richard Clay Ltd (The Chaucer Press)
Bungay, Suffolk

Contents

Preface

This book is about the social and religious life of a very small minority of people: single women. Our society, in which the great majority of women are married, imposes on those who are not the need to discover, or even to invent for themselves, their own identity and philosophy of life. Searching, as all human beings do, for happiness and self-respect, establishing themselves in relationships with other people, single women find that most of society's traditional wisdom is simply not addressed to them, just as the road signs on the motorway are not addressed to pedestrians or yachtsmen.

Religion is more than personal faith, or activities within a church; it concerns the whole of life, our social environment, and all that goes to make up the self, either in solitude or in the totality of one's relationships. It means the process by which we identify the objects (which include people), the activities and values which make our lives worth living, either in the sense of making us happy, or bringing about a state of mind in which unhappiness is endurable because it is not meaningless. It means the formation of beliefs about the universe, and one's place in it, and of principles to guide one's relationships with other people. In this sense, everyone has a religion, and though this book is written from the standpoint of a Christian believer, the same method could be used by those who hold other faiths and philosophies of life. I hope that both Christians and others will find something to interest them in my study of the ideology underlying the condition of single women in our society, and that they will be prompted to examine their own beliefs, and the expectations of society as they experience them, to discover how far these are helping them in living their own lives.

It will be obvious that this book owes a great deal to the teachings of the new feminist movement; not to mention this at the outset would be not only dishonest but ungrateful. I should emphasize, however, that I have not repeated the opinions of others without applying them to my own experience, and most feminist writing so far has drawn on the experience of married women. I should also say that I was well into my thirties before I encountered any feminist teaching, and when I did so I felt (like many other women) that I was only hearing views expressed which I had long held in private, and that some long-standing mental conflicts, some of which went back to before I left school, were beginning to resolve themselves. I began to think about my situation as a single woman from both the Christian and the feminist point of view at the same time, which proved a much more illuminating process than doing so separately.

The result was not that I came to question any of the basic truths of the Christian faith, neither did I come to feel any better qualified to tell others how to lead a Christian life, and so this book does not contain any revisions of the creed or exhortations to piety. I did come, however, to understand why my religious self has strongly, consistently, and for a long time rejected most of what I was taught concerning the proper role of women in society in general and in the Christian community in particular. It might well be thought that a single woman who professes Christianity has a better chance than the non-Christian single woman of developing a satisfactory personal philosophy, and that one who is a member of a church has a better chance of establishing a secure social identity. Believing that this is generally true, I have nevertheless come to think that Christian belief and practice today not only neglect the religious life of the single woman, but in some ways actually pervert it.

Besides drawing on experience, my own and that of other women, I tried to find out from published literature, both Christian and non-Christian, how an unmarried woman should live today. I do not claim to have read all that has been written on the subject; in fact I deliberately confined myself to recent material that was readily available in libraries and bookshops, and on church bookstalls. On a few occasions I was able to attend discussion groups which touched on the same subject.

At times this search for the views of other people proved a depressing task; I read and heard many things which made me thank God I had not done so ten years earlier when I might have been naïve enough to believe them. I am now perfectly convinced that many otherwise good and wise people do not know the first thing about women, which is that they are not all alike, nor the second thing, which is that they are not all as men would like them to be. The portrayal of single women in the media (and, it must be admitted, in some feminist literature), showed a 'grab what you can while you can' mentality that is easily exploited, and therefore cultivated, by those who expect to make money or to take sexual advantage of women who may appear emancipated but are in fact desperately lonely and lacking in self-control. And every time I met or heard about other single women who live under the same conditions as I do, yet bear them without my impatience, and still show forth so much more love and sound practical achievement than I do, I felt that they were succeeding where I am failing, but I still wanted to puzzle out just *why* I was so dissatisfied.

In view of the fact that I have criticized other writers fairly severely, I ought to say that even the works I found most objectionable deserve some credit for treating this badly neglected subject at all. I found examples of what I consider to be extremely rigid and inhuman morality, and of morbid and hysterical piety, but one must respect authors' convictions, and if they believe that a single woman can solve her problems by becoming more moral and more pious they have every right to say so. On the practical level, for example on home-making, one can find plenty of good advice, and some of the treatment of personal and psychological matters is very well worth reading – for example, Shelagh Brown on relationships with parents, or Margaret Evening on lesbian friendship. It is in the dimension of what I understand as religious life in the widest sense, the nature and vocation of the single woman and her place in society and the church, that I did not find satisfactory answers to the questions I was asking.

I hope to contribute by this book to greater understanding between the Christian community and the feminist movement. Many feminists have only the most superficial knowledge of the gospel, and have been alienated from Christianity by the exceptionally bad record of some churches in their dealings with women. Many Christians appear to know nothing of feminism beyond what they learn from the media, which concentrate on its more sensational aspects, and often create the impression that feminists are 'mad, bad and dangerous to know'.

This book is written as propaganda. It could not have been written any other way. My first aim has been to express a point of view, that of a single woman. It is so seldom that this point of view finds expression that it seemed more important to state it clearly than to be scrupulously impartial towards other points of view, which already have their advocates. Inequality of social status between single and married people does not mean that their personal relationship is necessarily a bad one, and when it is, the fault may lie on either side. I am aware that improvement in the status of single women will require effort on their part, and changes of attitude, especially towards each other. Similarly, I know that men also, particularly single men, also suffer social disadvantages, and that no individual man can be held responsible for the social disadvantage suffered by single women. From a religious point of view it is important to evaluate rights and responsibilities in the social system, but it is much more important to realize that this cannot even be attempted until we stop confusing the social system with 'human nature' or, worse still, the 'will of God'.

Finally, this book is noticeably lacking in the spirit of meekness, in the willingness to endure frustration and even injustice for Christ's sake. It has seemed to me, however, that before one can give oneself to God's service one must have some real authentic self to give, and that if one is to endure evil as a true Christian, one must first be able to recognize it for what it is. I think there may be many Christian single women who are in revolt against their condition, and aware that they are being dehumanized by it, without realizing that neither they personally, nor God, are entirely to blame, and so are living under a burden of quite unnecessary guilt, as I once did.

I very much regret that I was not able to explore aspects of single life beyond my own experience, such as the situation of the ex-wife, the single mother and the lesbian. Nothing I say should be taken as meaning that I think any woman's chances for a happy or a Christian life are better in single life than in marriage, or vice versa. I have not attempted to deal with individual reactions to singleness, but hope that much of what I say may be applied to both the ex-wife and the permanently single woman, the heterosexual and the homosexual, to the woman who wishes to marry and the one who does not, and the one who is not sure about it.

It is still very much my personal point of view, however, and my perception of even the social aspects of single life will certainly differ from that of other single women. I hope that many more will express their own points of view in public. I should add that no one among my family or friends, or in any church to which I have belonged, is responsible for any of my opinions or the words I choose to express them. I should like, however, to acknowledge that I received general encouragement, and helpful comments, for which I am very sincerely grateful, from the following: Stuart Burns, Phil Croft, Pauline Ford, Kay Gibbons, Alan and Sue Gray, Chris Oldman, Claire Wilkie, Bill, Joyce and Jane Williams, Erica Wright. My thanks are also due to the Revd John Stacey, of Epworth Press, for his help and advice, and to the University of Leeds for granting me leave of absence in order to prepare the book.

Leeds 1980   MARGARET BRITTON

I | *The single woman in a society founded on marriage*

'Unnatural' and 'abnormal' are very difficult words for
members of our common culture to face. They are the
equivalent for our age of what 'damned' meant to our
ancestors in the Age of Faith' (Elizabeth Janeway, *Man's
World, Woman's Place*).

Some years ago I had a short but significant conversation with a
middle-aged American widow in the bus station at Salinas, Cali-
fornia. After chatting pleasantly to me for some minutes, she
remarked that it was nice that young people like me had the chance
to travel and to see the world. Then suddenly she gave me a sharp
look and said: 'I suppose you would be about twenty-six, would
you?' 'No,' I replied, 'I'm thirty-four.' With an even sharper look
she enquired: 'Why aren't you married at your age?'

This incident is typical; nearly every single woman I know, including some much younger than myself, has been asked this
question in some form or other. To be single is something one
has to account for. Unmarried people do not belong to a definable
social group – such as being a Londoner or a BA or a Christian –
they cannot point to a common factor in their lives that explains
why they are single, they must give explanations based on their
personal history as individuals. Nor can they point to a common
aim in life for which being single is a requirement. They are an
anomaly in a society founded on marriage. To be single is to
attract the attention of other people, not merely as observers but
as judges. Like the criminal and the saint, the single person
inhabits a moral dimension, arousing curiosity, pity, scorn, envy
or admiration. Being single is not just unusual, it is abnormal, and
in our society this word is always value-laden and usually pejora-
tive.

This condition of single life, abnormality in the social sense, is
recognized by all the writers on this subject I have so far encountered, but (with the exception of the handful of feminist writers)

only in so far as they state more or less explicitly that a sense of being 'odd', and of experiencing the negative attitudes of other people, may contribute to a feeling of disillusionment, regret and resentment in women who are dissatisfied with single life. They speculate very little, however, as to why single life should be considered abnormal in the first place, and, even more strangely, they take for granted that it will be unsatisfactory only for women. There is no consideration of the subject from the point of view of single men, or even of single people in general. The purpose of the traditionalist writers is to counter these negative feelings by advising their women readers how to make the best of single life. It seems to me, however, that this omission seriously undermines the value of what they have to say; an understanding of the social aspects of the single woman's condition seems to me to be fundamental to understanding the more personal aspects.

Their approach to the subject, however, follows the general tendency of our society to treat the problems of women as *personal* problems, arising from the behaviour of individuals and their immediate family or neighbours, problems which are therefore seen to demand personal solutions, changes in attitude on the part of the individual. When put at its crudest, this means that if you as a woman are not content with your lot in life, there is something wrong with *you*. Women are usually brought up to think of themselves primarily as members of a small social group such as a family or a church, not as members of the total society in which they live. They are seldom encouraged to step back far enough from their problems to see how they are rooted not only in personal psychology but also in an economic and social system. Christians, too, are often taught to distrust any sense of personal injustice, and discontent is easily stigmatized as ingratitude towards God or other people. I wonder, indeed, if the social aspect of the single woman's condition may have been neglected by Christians through unconscious fear of uncovering anger against the 'powers that be'. A Christian woman can try to forgive known individual people who have done her wrong, but what can she do to forgive the whole of the society around her? There is nothing so destructive to the personality as anger combined with helplessness, and until very recently it was always assumed that women could do nothing to change society; they could only change themselves to fit in better. There is no need to perpetuate this assumption today.

By concentrating on the personal aspects, moreover, Christian writers give the impression that the Christian single woman lives in a state of insulation from the values of the secular world. Some write as if our society were still run on Christian principles, which is not the case, and others imply that Christians should associate only with one another, which is not only impossible but also contrary to Christ's teaching and example. It is not enough to say, and even genuinely to believe, that in God's sight marriage and single life are equally worthy. On earth they are not, and we do not and cannot ignore the views of those among whom we live, no matter how mistaken they may be. Whatever the theoretical teaching, in practice the inequality of status between single and married exists inside the Christian community as well as outside, which makes it all the more important that Christians should be aware of it.

Naturally, any member of a small minority must at times feel that he or she is an 'odd one out', and a woman who wished to marry and could not do so, or who did marry and had her marriage brought to an end, is likely to feel that she as an individual has not found her desired niche in society. This is not the same, however, as being aware of the social disadvantage of single women as a class. A sense of personal deprivation is a subjective state which varies in intensity with individual women, depending on how much they wish for marriage and its benefits. The social disadvantage of single women is an objective fact: *all* single women experience it, even those who are taking full advantage of the benefits of single life and are not sensitive to the attitudes of other people. The converse is also true: marriage and (even more) motherhood lend much dignity and social prestige even to those women who were never very enthusiastic in personal terms about becoming wives and mothers.

A small-scale example might be useful here. If a married woman says to me: 'I must get on home or Fred'll think I've been run over by a bus,' my reaction might be either to feel depressed at the thought that if I were run over by a bus it would be at least three days before anyone noticed, or to feel gleeful because I can stay out as late as I like without consulting any Fred. Which way I react depends on my personality, my individual attitude to marriage, and even perhaps on my mood at the time. But when she remarks on the awkwardness of seating an odd number of men and women at her table (yes, people do still say that sort of thing), I resent it because she is implying that people ought to go about in couples. It may even be true that discrimination against the single state is harder to bear for those who do *not* wish to be married. Those who do will find it easier to accept sympathy, and can feel that a definite solution to their problems exists, even though they may never achieve it. Those who have decided against marriage may come to feel that no solution exists, and are more easily made to feel that they are socially unacceptable. 'Why isn't a nice girl like you married?' (again, people do still say it), may comfort the one who wants to feel still eligible; to the one single by choice it sounds like an assertion that single girls aren't nice. Disparaging references to old maids, followed by a hasty 'but of course *you* aren't a spinster yet', do not encourage even the willingly single woman to think that her way of life is accepted as equal to marriage.

Even those who admit that social disadvantage exists – and in some forms, such as high taxation or the difficulties of single mothers, it can hardly be denied – and who accept as factual the accounts that any single woman can supply of exploitation, isolation and social exclusion, well-meaning interference of various kinds and outright sneering and slighting, usually go on to urge her not to be too sensitive. Surely it's only those who don't know any better who disparage single women, only the neanderthal man who thinks women exist to wash his dishes, or the smug little housewife just back from her honeymoon? If only this were true; but it seems to me that marriage and single life are not thought of as equal except among people who have given the matter long and serious thought, and that such people are very rare in the married majority. The social disadvantage of the single woman is founded not only on the opinions of stupid people whose views she can afford to ignore, but also on the opinions of people she loves and respects, and who exercise real power over her life. It is not only advertisements and pop songs and the like that tell her she is no good without a man, but also her family, her friends, her doctor, the minister of her church, the economic system and the whole culture in which she was reared. The tactful majority of people will be prepared to judge her to some extent on personal merit, but to the end of her days she will be thought of as happy or successful *in spite of* being single, whereas a wife is judged happy and successful until proved otherwise.

This is an age of rebellion, and it might be thought that omitting to become or remain married is a comparatively mild form of social deviancy. I am not so sure. To many single people, marriage seems too much like a lifelong commitment to social conformity, but the cost of social non-conformity in this sense must also be counted. Once married, it is not easy to revert to being single. The reverse process is not always easy either, and for some women it must remain impossible. A non-conforming life-style loses acceptability as the non-conformer grows older. Nor can one take time off from being single, as one might decide to take a rest from other forms of non-conformity, such as being a vegetarian, or a ban-the-bomb campaigner, or even a Christian. If you really believe in the value of the single state for you, you really are obliged to live out your belief for every moment of the day and night.

Perhaps most important in the reckoning is the fact that being single represents a non-conformity in *private* life, in matters relating to the universal intimate life of sex and the family. Non-conformists in political or publicly social aspects of life can rely on most of the people they know neither understanding nor caring what all the fuss is about, but one who deviates in private life is doing something that everyone is involved in and can react to. In this sense, though the actual forms of reaction may be more lenient, being single is like being homosexual. It is also similar in the sense that the reaction will be highly ambivalent, neither constant sympathy nor constant scorn, which would at least define one's role as victim or criminal, but a constantly varying mixture of both. A remark once made to a friend of mine: 'It must be rather fun to be single once you've got over the initial disgrace', shows a very common ambivalence between envy and pity with a touch of complacency.

This does not mean that one need be gloomy about single life taken as a whole. It offers enormous personal advantages, and many single people would not trade these for all the social advantage in the world. It is, however, just as impossible to make out a formal case for single life in the abstract as it is to make out a case for marriage in the abstract without taking into account the characters of individual husbands and wives. One cannot simply say that single people avoid the physical and mental stresses of marriage, or that they have a better chance to develop their individual talents and character, though all this may well be true, especially for women. Single life is not just the absence of a partner, and a doing without whatever marriage is thought to be. It is, just as much as marriage, a commitment to an unknown future, and to being changed by that future. Neither marriage nor single life should be judged on the emotional ups and downs of the first few years. The effects of living with oneself alone are likely to be just as far-reaching as the effects of adjusting to a partner.

Other writers, however, have already provided plenty of valuable ideas as to how one should use the personal freedom which is the essence of single life. The first half of this book is intended to restore a balance by showing how this personal freedom is in reality limited by social factors. It is an attempt to study some of the single woman's experience in her upbringing, her work, leisure, personal relationships and life in the church, to show how these may be adversely affected by being single in a marriage-based society.

2 | *Upbringing*

It is all too easy for children to learn simply to follow the crowd, to come to think of their lives as running along immovable rails, and of the society in which they live as a massive, uncontrollable force to which they have no option but to subjugate themselves' (J. P. White, *Towards a Compulsory Curriculum*).[1]

Personal deprivation and social disadvantage can, it is true, sometimes be hard to disentangle, and this is the case when one considers the upbringing and education of the single woman. The early social training of any woman is such that she will come to hope for marriage as desirable in itself, or at least think it is inevitable, thus creating the possibility of feeling deprived if she is not married. At the same time she is not only very badly prepared for single life but actually taught to dread it, which creates the first and perhaps the greatest social disadvantage she will have to face.

Other writers better qualified than myself have documented the ways in which a girl's upbringing prepares her to expect that her future will be primarily that of a wife and mother. Her working career, and any other forms of personal enterprise, will be chosen and conducted so as to fit in with the major tasks of making a home and looking after a family. At every stage in development the choices that girls can make are restricted by the assumption that this is what they need and want. The possibility of independent living is seldom even mentioned. Being permanently single, like being divorced, deserted or prematurely widowed, is one of the things you just don't expect to happen to *you*.

Much research has been done on the manner in which the accepted social roles of women and men are presented directly to children in textbooks, fiction, TV and so on. I have had the opportunity to supplement this by reading educational literature directed at teachers and parents, and in the course of seven years' working in an educational library I have come across only a handful of references to single life that could be construed as

even mildly favourable. Full length books on human development, careers guidance, social psychology, citizenship and sex
education commonly do not even mention the fact that some
adults are not married, and when they do, single life is often
linked to poor social or sexual adjustment or the 'breakdown of
the family'. A typical example is Cole and Hall's handbook
Psychology of Adolescence[2] which includes nine cases of people who
'failed to reach adulthood', all unmarried but one. A well-known
psychologist portrays single people as sexual misfits, not only
pathetic in themselves but underminers of the social order:

> Men and women are only fully themselves when related to each
> other. When such a relation is completely absent, as in the case
> of bachelors and spinsters, we expect that the isolated person
> will take on some of the characteristics of the opposite sex.
> Men living alone very often become fussy, old-maidish and
> soft; while solitary women exhibit a pseudo-masculine efficiency,
> a determined practical competence which they might expect or
> demand from a husband if only they had one.[3]

Even when these stereotypes are no longer unquestioned, single
life is still treated as a doubtful proposition. Jacky Gillott's text-
book *For Better, for Worse*, for example, gives a very fair picture of
the disadvantages of marriage as well as its benefits, but hints that
to reject it is the sign of a deficiency in personality:

> Those who enjoy the company of large groups of people, or
> find no need for deep relationships in their lives, may prefer
> other arrangements. But there is a special kind of tenderness
> and tolerance that can grow only out of the steady companion-
> ship of *two* people.[4]

From the same sources, I gather that most of the old dilemmas
about the formal education of girls are as far from being resolved
as ever. I left school twenty-odd years ago grossly unfitted for the
life I was to lead, because the better sort of education for girls
could then be obtained only in those schools which had 'high
standards' in the non-curricular realm as well. To do well
academically one was forced to learn to be a lady, and there's no
worse handicap for a single woman than being a lady. The time
I spent being lectured about dress (i.e. uniform) and deportment,
good manners and keeping away from boys, or taking part in, or

being made to watch, competitions in Latin translation, poetry-reading, gymnastics and piano-playing, and the subsequent awarding of prizes, would have been better spent in learning to cope with meals, mortgages, machinery, motoring, minor ailments and men. It would have done those of us who did marry no harm either to have learned these things, and we could all have got our A-levels just the same. There would be no problem in deciding whether to educate girls for marriage or a career, if schools would only eliminate the things that don't do either.

Girls may not be so ladylike now, and where we used to be told not to eat ice-cream in the street, now they probably tell them not to shoot dope in the street, but what emerges from the educational system is still, it appears, a potential wife. The findings of the National Child Development Study[5] showed that out of over 12,000 young people only 3% had decided not to marry, 6% were uncertain, and only 8% were willing to wait for marriage more than ten years. A Department of Education survey on *Fifth Form Girls: Their Hopes for the Future*,[6] carried out in 1972, found that out of about 2,000 girls 3% were considering single life, heavily outnumbered by 4% married or engaged and 29% definitely wishing to marry. Of course this leaves a majority still undecided, and such early decisions may not be permanent, but these figures suggest that single life is no more favourably regarded than it was in my own youth. My reading leads me to believe that children are now given a more realistic picture of marriage, but they are still not having single life presented to them as a valid alternative, with the same study of problems that may arise, and the resources available for overcoming them.

If the official processes of education remain silent, for the most part, about the possibility of independent living, this gap is filled by the unofficial education supplied by the popular media, folklore and uninhibited conversation. My experience of the cultural stereotyping of single women is that it is even more conservative – not to say barbarous than the stereotyping of women in general, and even more exaggerated in terms of 'either/or' thinking. The single woman is seen as either a nun or a whore: either downtrodden, fussy, prudish, opinionated and neurotic, or selfish, predatory, ruthless, extravagant and irresponsible. There may have been some shifting of the outlines of these images in recent years, but I am not sure that they are getting any less negative.

Persistence in a thankless job or dreary home life is now just as
likely to be seen as emotional immaturity or lack of enterprise,
rather than devotion to duty, and on the other hand the coming of
the so-called permissive society has strengthened the myth that a
woman not attached to one man is fair game for all. Everyone is
an amateur psychologist these days, and can detect the hidden
weakness and self-doubt behind individual heroism even at the
Florence Nightingale level (and not everyone wants to be a heroine while one of the meanings of 'heroine' is 'freak'). When a single
woman is portrayed as worthy of respect, it is still more often than
not as the collaborator of some male tycoon, politician, scholar or
criminal, and to gain affection she must still play the part of
honorary mother or sister to a man. A third image is that of the
witch, who bypasses the laws of church and state to gain control
over her own life, and helps other women to do the same. The
most common witch-image used to be that of the lesbian, but it
has been very appropriately extended to include the modern
feminist woman.

The most insidious myth, however, is that of the single woman
as freak, rejected by men because she repels them sexually. Granted
that most single women do consider themselves as attractive as
the average wife, and that some really ugly and disagreeable
women do find husbands, I think it still does not do to dismiss too
readily the effect of real or imaginary physical defects on the
individual's self-confidence. Girls are seldom allowed to grow up
entirely satisfied with their own bodies, no matter how beautiful
they are by nature, and much self-esteem is invested in time and
trouble (and money) spent on improving their natural looks by art,
to be repaid, it is hoped, by increased powers of attracting men.
A man will invest self-esteem in what he does, rather than how
he looks. In fact it is still possible to upset a man quite badly by
telling him he is beautiful! Since men are supposed to take the
initiative in courtship, a woman who is trying to find a husband
without success, even if she knows there is nothing wrong with
her mind or her manners, may come to think there is something
indefinably wrong with her body. If she has not yet found a man
that she can love, she may come to think that she is unlovable, or
'incapable of love' or some other phrase out of the less helpful
side of popular psychology.

Unhappily, this myth casts a shadow over the future too. Loss of
self-confidence can be the cause of defects as well as the result.

One can blame heredity for a big nose or the wrong height, but a woman who thinks herself unattractive can develop mannerisms that in fact make her so. One cannot entirely ignore the old superstition that marriage itself is essential for a woman to develop properly, that without it her mind and body will wither and go sour. A belief of this kind can become a self-fulfilling prophecy, especially if it is reinforced by the damaging and perfectly real effects of prolonged loneliness. If one then adds the effects of an upbringing that leads girls to believe that only as wives and mothers will what they do and say and think actually matter to somebody, it is hardly surprising that one of the incentives to marry is the fear of what staying single may do to you. Fear of being 'left on the shelf' is considered in a Scripture Union pamphlet published in 1972[7] to be experienced at the same level as fear of incurable illness, the death of parents, and war. All Christian writers I have read present this fear as being felt only by women. It is extraordinary how it persists in spite of demographic changes which make it likely that in future more men will remain single than women, not to mention the fact that happy and successful single women have existed in large numbers in any age.

Even allowing plenty of time for education and getting started in a career, very few women would not consider themselves of an age to marry by about twenty-four at the latest. It is very much harder to set an upper age limit, and most women are encouraged by family and friends to put off the acceptance of singleness as long as possible. This means that single women have spent a large part of their lives, ten years at least and sometimes much more, with an ambivalent identity, not sure whether they are in fact single women or prospective wives. I think that living with this ambivalence is much more difficult than most people realize, who have never tried it, and it certainly gets no easier with time. Once past the mid-twenties the life of the single woman really is different from that of the wife; their aims in life are not compatible. (For the ex-wife who has to change identities, it may be even more difficult.) Both the advantages and the disadvantages of single life become more obvious as time goes on. It is hard to take advantage of freedom while still hankering after security, to learn to profit from temporary relationships while still thinking of permanent ones as ideal, to live fully in the present and yet plan for a future that may be totally different, to conform to the norms of society while persistently breaking one of the most universal, and to adjust one's sexual attitudes to the possibilities of both monogamy and permanent abstinence.

The choice or acceptance of single life in our society represents a turning aside from the course of the majority, a stepping outside the conventions. At the worst it may bring with it a heavy blow to the self-confidence. At the best it is a setting out into largely unmapped territory. Why, then, are some women not married? Is it merely their fate, or their own decision, or their own fault, or does God decide this matter for us?

3 | *Vocations*

On February 7th, 1837, God spoke to me and called me to
His service (Florence Nightingale).

The idea of a vocation to single life is a very old one in Christian
tradition, and rests on the fact that freedom from the responsibilities of family life allows a woman to devote the whole of her
time and energy to God in prayer and some form of Christian
work. 'The unmarried woman cares for the Lord's business'
(I Cor. 7.34). A life thus dedicated is based on a vocation, literally the call of God to perform some particular task. The woman
so called feels that she has been chosen by God for something
that she alone can and must do, and that by accepting this call
she gains access to the grace needed to carry it out. Such a woman
also feels 'singled out' in the sense that her vocation makes
marriage impossible, or reduces her chances of finding a husband
to the point at which expecting to marry is unrealistic, or fulfils
her emotional needs in a way that makes marriage superfluous.
Until fairly recently it also usually meant that the woman joined
some kind of organized enterprise such as a mission or a religious
order. It does not necessarily follow, even in the traditional teaching, that celibacy (in the sense of sexual abstinence) and the
sacrifice of the benefits of marriage are in themselves pleasing to
God, but this is an idea which has always been closely associated
with the idea of vocation to single life. Paul's next words in the
verse quoted above are: 'her aim is to be dedicated to him in body
as in spirit.'

No doubt women are still to be found who 'renounce marriage
for the sake of the kingdom of Heaven' (Matt. 19.12), but it is
not hard to see why their numbers are declining. Among Protestants at least it appears to be assumed that the eventual vocation
of all women is marriage:

Training young people for marriage – and that must begin as
soon as the child begins to be aware of the behaviour of adults
– is an essential part of the Christian task.[1]

The need to sacrifice marriage to 'the Lord's business' is also being eroded by the fact that it is becoming easier for a woman to combine marriage, and bringing up children, with a full-time and lifelong career. Not so long ago, in my mother's generation, a woman had to be single to enter or remain in a vocational profession such as teaching. Today, becoming a teacher or a nurse or even a missionary does not necessarily involve renouncing marriage, and institutional support for the dedicated celibate has declined as a result. Though Christians may still admire a dedicated single woman, they do not as a rule really understand her motives, and so can do little to strengthen her in the inevitable times of weariness and doubt. The Christian vocation *par excellence*, the priesthood, though it does not invariably entail a vow of celibacy, is in some churches still closed to women altogether.

It is not difficult either to see why, in the early days of Christianity, a woman who wanted to serve God in any other way than through her family and home, had to renounce both and remain single. Quite apart from religious considerations as to the merits of celibacy, it would not have been practicable for her to combine marriage with a vocation. The differences in the daily life of the single woman and the wife are still considerable, but they used to be very much greater, and so tradition has established in our minds that a certain spiritual vocation is linked with a certain marital status. Conversely, one could not, in former times, choose to remain single without adopting the way of life of the dedicated celibate. Religious vocation still remains one of the respectable reasons for being single; even in non-religious thinking the single state of some individual in public life, such as a politician or an actress, is 'explained' by saying that she is 'wedded to her career'. Now that single women are in such a small minority and declared vocations rarer still, we are even more hard put to it to find reasons for why single women are as they are. Traditionalist Christian writers appear to be trying to fill this vacuum by returning to the idea of single life as a vocation, but expressing it in reverse form: that God keeps some women single in order that they may serve him in a different way. This is a disastrous setting of the cart before the horse.

Widening the context to examine the choices open to all Christians as they decide how to spend their lives, there seems to me to be a fundamental choice in practice between two alternatives: the life of a pro-Creator, where Adam tills the ground and

Eve brings up the next generation, and the life of a pro-Redeemer, who turns her or his back on home and family, and on security of any kind, to preach and minister and fight and suffer for the kingdom of God. It is hard not to make the second choice sound superior, but that is no reason for disparaging the first. The text of Micah: 'What doth the Lord require of thee, but to do justly, and to love mercy, and to walk humbly with thy God?' (Micah 6.8) has been described by Mary McCarthy as 'the authentic voice of Protestantism'.[2] Another writer (to whom I owe much besides this) points out that the doctrine expressed in Micah's words:

> While it admits all sorts of perplexity and hesitation and failure, it altogether excludes the view that my life has no purpose, that there is no reason why I am here, that what I do does not matter.[3]

Lack of a specific vocation does not mean lack of grace to serve God, nor does it necessarily mean that one's 'true' vocation is marriage.

It seems to me of the utmost importance that the choice between these two ways of life should be decided by the talents and conscience of the individual, the gifts and the voice of the Spirit within them, rather than by their sex or marital status. As things are at present, it is too easily assumed that for a woman life as a pro-Creator means marriage and motherhood, while life as a pro-Redeemer goes with staying single. I do not see why any woman who feels called to the pro-Creator role should not choose Adam's work rather than Eve's, following a lifelong career of useful work, but not in the sense of being dedicated to a specific task, or even to a particularly 'Christian' type of work. If she faces difficulties in doing Adam's work without any of Adam's privileges in the world of work, this is still a better choice than forcing herself into the pro-Redeemer role for no better reason than being single.

I find it impossible to believe, as some do, that God actually causes a woman to remain single against her own choice, and that the fact of being single constitutes a vocation to anything. God may, in some cases, and particularly in response to prayer, grant a personal vocation to one who is single for any reason, but this is something that God chooses to do, we cannot choose for him. We must at all costs avoid the assumption that a personal vocation exists, or will automatically come into being, once the only recognized alternative, marriage, has not happened by the time the woman turns thirty or so. The evil spectre of the Christian spinster performing her Good Works in a spirit of condescension and unhealthy religiosity, and often very incompetently as well, will never be exorcized until the good works are undertaken as an honest alternative choice, not merely to justify her existence after 'failure' to marry.

I believe that very few single women can be absolutely certain whether their single state is due to outward circumstances, to subconscious psychological factors, or to a conscious decision, and that the distinction is not as important as it might seem. It could be important for an individual single woman, especially if her singleness is making her chronically unhappy, to find out whether she is being prevented from marrying by some hidden hang-up, but this will certainly be more easily done if she is conscious of the social factors as well. In the next chapter I consider some of the social and temperamental factors that might be involved. For the minority who have received a call from God, such considerations will be irrelevant. A vocation to celibacy is a vocation *to* celibacy for a purpose, not merely a vocation *against* marriage. God may ask us to do things for him that at first sight seem impossible, but in all cases of vocation of which I ever heard there was an impulse *towards* some course of action, though it might at first seem quite unnatural:

> This appalling idea of religious vocation simply settled itself in my mind . . . there was no alternative. I had to go forward along this way that was now so painfully clear.[4]

One can sympathize to some extent with the motives of those who urge single women to aspire to sainthood, and to believe that God has caused or allowed them to be single as part of his purpose for their lives. It is certainly better than believing that he has forsaken them altogether. I think they are very much mistaken, however, in assuming that the only alternative to the belief in singleness as a vocation must be despair. The words of Jesus quoted at the head of the next chapter show that he is very well aware of the distinction between those whose vocation requires them to be single, 'for whom God has appointed it', and those who are single for other reasons. Even a genuine vocation has its spiritual dangers, and such a belief intensifies them for women who are only trying to convince themselves that God has caused them to be single. Those whose single state is for them a source of feelings of failure and deprivation may try to manufacture a vocation to free themselves of guilt and enhance their status with other people. Those who see it in terms of freedom and independence may develop too much pride in their own abilities, and think of themselves as superior to the common herd in spiritual as well as in other ways.

By implying that women's marital status is none of their own choosing, a belief in singleness as a vocation in itself encourages women to abdicate responsibility for choice in other areas of life as well. Worst of all, it imposes a very limited view of the possible roles of women, by attaching such overwhelming significance to their earthly relationships with men.

4 | *Choices*

> The disciples said to him, 'If that is the position with
> husband and wife, it is better not to marry.' To this he
> replied 'That is something which not everyone can accept,
> but only those for whom God has appointed it. For while
> some are incapable of marriage because they were born so,
> or were made so by men, there are others who have
> themselves renounced marriage for the sake of the kingdom
> of Heaven. Let those accept it who can' (Matt. 19.10–12).

Neither marriage nor single life is made entirely in heaven, though
one can still find those who are naïve enough to think so:

> If God leads you into it [i.e. marriage] it will be wonderful. If
> he doesn't it means that he has something different in mind,
> which for you will be far better.[1]

All good things come from God, but most of them reach us
through the agency of other people. God's first gift, life itself, can
reach us only by means of two other human beings who cause
us to be born, and throughout our lives we continue to receive
his gifts partly by direct experience but chiefly through people
who love us and work for us and teach us. It is a wonderful thing
that human beings can co-operate with God, but in accepting this
we must also accept that they can hinder God's will and prevent
its fulfilment, and that man has created situations in which women
whose vocation it is to marry cannot do so. Some have been so
undermined in their self-confidence, or made to be so ashamed of
their sexuality, that they turn away from marriage, some have
been placed in isolated homes or jobs where they cannot find a
partner, some fall in love with a man who can't or won't marry
them and are unable to commit themselves to anyone else. Some
have been hurt and appalled by disastrous marriages they have
known, either their own or perhaps those of family or friends.

 One of the most curious twists of the belief in singleness as a
vocation is its implication that only marriage as a vocation can be
welcomed by the recipient. A vocation to singleness is seen as a

good thing only in spiritual terms. The possibility that it might be the natural inclination of some women, and that fulfilling it does not necessarily mean subduing nature, does not seem to attract much attention. The existence of homosexuality in women is ignored by the majority of Christian moralists, and so are other ways in which a woman may be 'incapable of marriage by nature'.

I have noticed that single people include a high proportion of both extremely introvert and extremely extrovert people, that is, those who are naturally solitary and those who are naturally convivial, those who need plenty of time alone, and those who need a great variety of friends rather than intensely intimate relationships. The convivial temperament is supposed to be more common in men than women, and is certainly better catered for by the custom of masculine social drinking and sport and so on, but it also exists in a minority of single women. The naturally solitary woman is a victim of one of the all-or-nothing choices so characteristic of women's lives in our society; nobody has less solitude than the wife with young children. Those who cannot do without it – and it is one of life's greatest blessings – are forced to live under the perpetual threat of one of life's greatest evils, loneliness.

Some women, too, lack the 'subordinate talents'. They are deficient in the practical skills of home-making or the psychological skills of family life, or at any rate have no desire to practise these skills full-time. It is one thing to cook a good meal occasionally, and another to make oneself entirely responsible for the nourishment of several other people; it is one thing to pour oil on troubled waters in an emotional crisis, and another to expect to have to cope with every domestic friction for years to come. Since the ideal wife was invented by men, no real woman ever quite comes up to her, and some women would prefer not to have to live with this failure day by day for the rest of their lives. Some women object to marriage as an institution on perfectly sincere grounds of principle. Then there are those whose sexual and maternal drives are weak, or weak in comparison with other drives such as the longing for achievement in their work, for fame or travel or danger. Just how far God enters into the formation of such temperaments is an open question, but to call them a 'vocation' in the traditional sense is quite obviously absurd.

In their eagerness to praise God's providence, it is all too easy

for Christians to obliterate all trace of the part played by the
whole community in the formation of a marriage. Even the man
is seen as passive, and the woman is seldom recommended to do
anything but watch and pray:

> Have you ever thought that if you permit God to work, He'll
> make you into just the right woman for the man He's picked
> out for you? How many times do we Christians miss out in
> our lives because we charge after something that looks like the
> real thing and manage to miss the extraordinary thing God was
> arranging![2]

In this as in other decisions in life, God gives women enterprise
and judgment so that they may seek out 'the real thing', and
whether it turns out real or not, responsibility rests partly with the
woman herself. Faith in God and prayer for help in finding a husband is one thing, total passivity is another. The same writer and
others hold up as examples the women of the Bible who waited for
God to order their marital destiny. It seems to me thoroughly dishonest to do this without admitting that such women were subject
to the will of other people, chiefly their fathers, and the customs
of their society. In our society, women have the option of remaining single; if they wish to marry they carry a large share of
responsibility for finding their husbands for themselves. Plenty
of social constraints still operate in our society, however, which
restrict the choice of possible partners: age, class, race, geographi-
cal situation, and so on. The issue cannot be reduced to a direct
confrontation or partnership between the will of God and the
will of an individual woman. Other people are always involved
as well.

Some writers include advice to the single woman on how to
find a husband, but it very seldom amounts to more than how to
be where potential husbands might be met with. There is never
any suggestion that a woman can or should take the initiative in
courtship, and where more formal procedures such as a marriage
bureau are mentioned, it is with vague warnings of unspecified
danger. For the most part the single woman is merely encouraged
to deserve marriage by cultivating the virtues of a good prospective wife. This links up with another limiting factor in the single
woman's choices, which is that in our society it is considered a
bad omen for a marriage if the wife is better educated than her
husband, or more successful in terms of money or status. This

convention has weakened in the recent past, but it would still be thought odd for a woman to say openly that she was not looking for high earning power or intelligence in her future partner, but would prefer such qualities as sympathy or physical attractiveness. Single women are constantly warned that they must not compete with men if they want to please them, and the qualities that make for worldly success are still thought of as 'manly'. The American sociologist Jessie Bernard, in her book *Academic Women*,[3] used this convention as foundation for her hypothesis that very clever women and very stupid men are the most likely people to have difficulty in marrying. This is only partly disproved by the existence of many marriages between clever women and stupid men. I think it has some validity in that older single women and single men often seem to have much less in common than one might expect, to have other mental differences besides those directly caused by difference of sex. She also makes a link between intellectual and physical stature, pointing out that very few men will marry a woman taller than themselves, so that many single women are over the average in height and weight, and many single men below it. The husband must have physical superiority too!

With the very high marriage rates of today, any woman not married by the age of twenty-five stands a high statistical chance of never marrying at all.[4] The divorce rate is also high, but this may not be much help to Christians who have scruples about marriage to a divorced man, and many divorces take place only when one or both partners have a second partner already lined up. This being so, though one can sympathize with the motives of those who try to encourage young people to delay marriage until their mid-twenties (such as a university chaplain who told me that he made a point of never congratulating students on their engagements, and never allowed his premises to be used for social events that required guests to have a partner), it should perhaps be more clearly understood that a decision to marry late means a restricted choice of partners; and the possibility of permanent singleness must be accepted whether or not one considers it God's will!

The chances of a Christian marriage, that is, marriage to a Christian husband, are even lower. Most churches retain the allegiance, at least so far as attending services and social events is concerned, of far more single women than single men, and so are not in a position to give practical help to an older single woman who wants to marry a Christian. This being so, perhaps they ought not to be so ready to condemn marriage to a non-Christian. Shelagh Brown, in *Single: Fulfilment and the Single Christian Woman*, goes so far as to say that women who have refused to consider marrying a non-believer can claim to have 'renounced marriage for the sake of the kingdom of Heaven'. She states that Christian women outnumber Christian men by two to one, and possibly three or four to one in the older age groups, and though she quotes no evidence for this my own experience suggests that it may well be true. If so, it is high time someone found out the reason for it, since it suggests that there is something very much amiss in the way the Christian community deals with men. Meanwhile, though marriage between Christians and non-Christians will bring obvious difficulties, this attitude is highly objectionable. It encourages the ghetto mentality, making Christians cut themselves off from the world around them, instead of going out to meet it and showing that Christ is for everybody, not just a select few. People who marry without first discovering their partners' attitudes and values, not only about God but also about education, politics, sex and money, are asking for trouble anyway. Whatever the case regarding marriage, Christ is not well served, and we will not bring people to know him, by referring to non-believers as 'spiritually dead' (Andrews), 'unsaved' (Sands) or to 'mixed marriages' as inevitably bringing 'disaster' (Burbridge).

5 | *Work*

It is after all going to be a long time before the men's world
of business becomes anything like a people's place of work.
Millions of women will spend an entire career life living
and working in a culture whose traditions, rules and
implicit codes are derived from the male experience
(M. Hennig and A. Jardim, *The Managerial Woman*).

I find it strange that the subject of work has attracted relatively
little attention from Christian writers on the single woman's situation. Most single women have full-time jobs, and whatever their
attitude to their work, it occupies a very high proportion of their
time and energy. It should certainly have received more consideration from those who believe that to be single is in itself a
vocation, for unless a woman has a private income, or joins some
community that will provide for her material needs, a vocation to
God's work must be expressed through a paid job sought in the
normal employment market. Those who do not have a vocation
of the traditional kind, and are seeking a vocation *in* single life
rather than *to* it, will still meet with plenty of problems in trans-
lating their desire to use their talents in God's service into actually
fitting themselves into the secular world of work. Christian
writers generally recognize, however, that a good job can be an
important means of self-development and a source of satisfaction
for a single woman. One writer, Janice Glover in *Sense and
Sensibility for Single Women*, who does treat the subject of work at
some length, lists the following requirements for a satisfactory
job: that it should provide financial security, companionship, an
outlet for creativity, a purpose in life and some degree of social
status.

Women's employment is a very complex subject, and conditions in it are changing with astonishing speed. A satisfactory
study of single women at work today would demand abilities that
neither I nor previous writers on the subject possess. Some consideration of it is needed, however, because it is one of the most
important of the social factors that affect the single woman's life.

It is in fact an area where choice can be very restricted; the Christian often has to bow to necessity, and this may be unacceptable to those Christians who want to attribute all life's events to God's providence. This can be specially true of older single women, since many girls choose work that pays well at the start, without considering its future prospects, or limit themselves to the few careers that can be easily combined with family life. By the time they realize they may be permanently single, most women will have been working for ten years at least, for the ex-wife there may have been a long interval without paid work at all, and a change to a rewarding career may simply not be possible. Men, who expect to work throughout their lives, have the incentive to take their careers seriously right from the start, and are more likely to receive appropriate education and training.

There is of course a vicious circle at work here: women are thought more likely to abandon their jobs for family reasons than men are, so employers and others are less willing to invest in their education and training. This results in low earnings and uninteresting work and gives women an incentive to opt for family life instead. It is important to remember also that being single is an expensive way to live. For many women it is completely out of reach for economic reasons, or economically less desirable than marriage.

It is encouraging that so much is now being done to reduce the disadvantage of women in employment, particularly in helping girls to find work in a wider range of jobs than those traditionally thought suitable for women. But while those starting work today are restricted by the general shortage of work for everyone, those who started work more than about fifteen years ago may not be much affected by these improvements. The majority of employed women are still in the traditional women's professions: teaching, nursing and social work, or in 'service' jobs such as clerical work, selling and catering. There are still very few women in the highly skilled trades (which are also the highly paid ones), or in the high-status professions such as law, medicine, pure science and finance.

Some single women, I know, also feel that current efforts to improve the conditions and prospects of working women are benefiting mainly the increasing numbers of married women workers, while single women, who are more usually sole breadwinners for themselves and others, are merely losing what advantages they once had. The working spinster is being written off as a relic of past ages:

> I am taking it for granted that we all start from the basic assumption that, in modern society, it is both desirable and necessary for women to play a dual role. The great band of spinsters who used to do so much of the essential work is now as extinct as the dodo, and a good thing too.[1]

Some of us are far from extinct and likely to have to go on working for twenty years or more, hindered to some extent by the handicaps, such as inadequate education, that we started off with, and does this sort of thinking really take into account the increasing number of single mothers who work to keep themselves and their children?

The traditional view of women's work, that it involves attendance on the needs and wants of other people, rather than making decisions or material goods, and should be rewarded by personal fulfilment (whatever that is) rather than money or status, is reinforced by Christian thinking. As long ago as 1946 an interesting pamphlet by W. G. Symons, *Work and Vocation*, stated that Christians tended to have a mental value-scale by which working directly for the church was seen as most worthy, the 'caring' professions such as education and medicine came second, then the other professions, with jobs in ordinary commerce and industry last of all. It seems quite a fair summary of Christian attitudes even today. The institutional interest of the Christian community in employed women is still concentrated on the traditional womanly careers, and within them on the professions. It is much easier to find advice on being a Christian teacher than a Christian typist, and one hears very little about the Christian woman as accountant or machine-minder. Single women may also be channelled into a narrow range of work by getting the idea that service jobs are a protection against loneliness because they involve 'dealing with people'.

Symons goes on to say that 'ordinary' commerce and industry are the field in which the real moral and social struggles of our time are going on, and that Christians are needed there as much as anywhere. This is even more true today, and one of the said struggles is the attempt of working women to gain more control over their own lives, and a greater voice in the decisions they work to implement. Support from the Christian community should be reaching not only those women whose hard work keeps the wheels of our society turning, but also those who are dissatisfied with the direction in which those wheels are running, and who are trying to reach the policy-making level both in management and in the trade unions. This struggle is now spreading to the vocational professions as well, involving more women than ever. If Christian women workers are to be a Christian influence in the world of work, they must also be supported in their efforts to make themselves heard as women.

When women do achieve power in the world of work, it is to be hoped that they will do something to change its nature. Another vicious circle has been set up by the fact that all rewards of ambition have been designed to appeal to men rather than women, so that women do not have the same incentives to reach the top of the hierarchy, and doing so often means abandoning the kind of behaviour that we have been taught to think of as feminine. Women often have great difficulties to face when trying to reconcile their personal values with those of a work organization. This does not mean that the organizational values are necessarily better. When, for example, one hears that women are too easily swayed by their emotions, what this really means is that they are more so than men, but it is men who have decided to what extent emotional considerations are to be allowed to influence the policy of an organization. While men control the world of work, and married women control the 'feminine' world of the home, the single woman has little opportunity in either for reaching a status of respect.

Single women at work also encounter discrimination against single people in general, which though less well documented is none the less real. I have even heard it said that if not supporting dependants they should be paid less for the same work. Ever since we discovered the powerful effects of repressed sexuality, the possibility of discrimination on grounds of emotional immaturity or instability, besides that of real or suspected homosexuality, has never quite dropped out of sight. I found two recent references to it in *The Shy Person's Book* by C. Rayner and *Interaction in the Classroom* by S. Delamont.[2] Some people think that if such discrimination exists, it is likely to be compounded by economic factors. The worker whose finances and mobility are limited by a family is less likely to cause trouble with an employer. It is commonly believed that a man increases his chances of promotion by getting married.

Some single people certainly are exploited by their employers in matters such as frequent transfers involving a change of dwelling-place, overtime at short notice and in excessive amounts, restriction of holidays to awkward times of year, and unwanted sexual advances. By this last I do not mean scuffles behind the filing-cabinet, but lonely people being exploited by charm laid on with an ulterior motive, as when a former colleague said to me of an older single woman, 'She'll do what we want if I smile at her and upset her hormone balance.'

I have the impression, too, that single people of both sexes do in fact tend to be less satisfied with their jobs, or at least more ready to complain, than married people are. Perhaps they complain more publicly because they have no one at home to hear out their grumbles. But many married people also find their work unrewarding; it could be that their responsibility, and social status, as breadwinners for other people helps them to put up with the disadvantages. Those who work only to keep themselves can more easily come to feel that neither they nor the job are worth the trouble. Since many single people do have fewer financial commitments than the married, they easily become more conscious of other aspects of the job besides the salary. Since they are also very heavily taxed, many reach a point where a higher salary counts for little in take-home pay, and they become more interested in other forms of reward for their work.

While it is obviously good policy for a single woman to make the most of her career, and Janice Glover may be right in suggesting that a good job can offer some of the same benefits as a good marriage, it is also true that most high-status, interesting and fulfilling jobs go to men, and even they seldom find them so fulfilling that they are willing to do without family life. In most career structures ambition involves being willing to change one's residence, and I know several single people, men included, who have abandoned their chances of promotion because they did not want to face building up a circle of friends all over again. Promotion can also mean class mobility, and (particularly, I think, for women) setting oneself apart from childhood friends and even family. The world of work has been designed to fulfil one set of needs in human beings, and the world of home another. There are very few jobs left that can in any way be used as a substitute for some kind of private personal life, and today, single people who commit their whole life and energy to their work run the risk of being completely dehumanized. Janice Glover does in fact warn her readers against over-dedication to work – and I note that she is in the same profession as myself (librarianship) where it can indeed have disastrous results on the personality! Most of the single people I know, men as well as women, have other commitments in their lives which they value as much or more than their paid work, and most are definitely less ambitious than their married colleagues.

6 | *Leisure*

We change singles into couples. We are now well known as
a company that makes meeting people of the opposite sex
as inevitable as getting an all over sun tan (Advertisement
for a 'singles holiday').

The traditional view of women's work extends also to voluntary
work, both in the fact that women are expected to do it and in
the nature of the tasks allotted to them. The role of the Christian
single woman as doer of Good Works dates from a time when
middle- and upper-class women (and most never-married women
are middle- and upper-class even today, for economic reasons)
did not have full-time jobs, so that voluntary work was an outlet
for unused talents as well as surplus energy – they did not do all
their own housework either. I sometimes wonder whether, in the
changed circumstances of today, it is not rather excessive to ask a
woman who spends all day in paid service to other people in one
of the traditional women's jobs, to spend her leisure doing the
same sort of thing unpaid. Many do, some to the extent of seem-
ing hardly ever to do anything else. Is there perhaps some unconscious attempt to be like the married woman worker who
spends her 'leisure' time caring for her family? Do women feel
guilty if they are not working?

The Christian community could set an example, in the very wide
range of voluntary work which it controls, of reducing the mis-
use and under-use of women's capabilities in our society. I do not
mean by this to accuse the churches of using women only as tea-
makers and brass-polishers and flower-arrangers, but this is an
impression that any outsider might quite reasonably acquire, for
the successes of women in positions of responsibility and influence need to have greater publicity. The ethics of voluntary work
are very complicated and I admit to having become somewhat
confused on the subject. No doubt the most important issue is
that the work which needs doing should somehow be done.
Where single women are concerned, however, it has seemed to
me that some organizers of voluntary work are not concerned

enough that the work is being done by those who have the necessary time and abilities, that it should be shared out fairly, made
as enjoyable as possible, and – most important – be worth doing
in the first place. Some really worthwhile work is being hampered by being done by overtired or incompetent people, and
work of another kind is often organized to 'help', or at least
occupy the spare time of, lonely and unhappy people whose
problems really demand a more radical solution.

Those who choose to remain single are sometimes stigmatized
as selfish and irresponsible people who want to spend all their
spare time and money on themselves. For a woman, indeed, to
be single is the only way she can be absolutely sure of having any
time or money of her own; some wives even in this day and age
have none at all. The typical single woman, however, is not the
lady of wealth and leisure that seems to exist in the minds of some
organizations that set out to cater for single people, or as portrayed in the media. Now that so many wives work, single people
have lost much of their former financial advantage. They have to
buy and furnish a home, for example, on one salary instead of two,
and they cannot count on help from family and friends as a married couple can. As a friend said to me: 'Marriage ought not to
be the only occasion in life to be celebrated with festivities and
showers of presents. My reaction to seeing requests for cutlery
sets as wedding presents is to ask whether the state of singleness
involves eating with your fingers, and one only evolves a more
civilized approach on marriage!'

Strange as it may seem, I think being single puts one at a disadvantage not only in earning money but in spending it, and in
the use of the leisure one has earned. Our society still shows a
strongly puritanical streak, not only in matters concerning sex,
but also concerning time and money, and in this light the single
person can appear greedy and even immoral. Isn't there something wickedly extravagant about a washing-machine or a deep-
freeze bought to be used by only one person? Yet when one thinks
of the time saved by the married man whose wife does his cooking,
shopping, cleaning, hostessing and keeping up social ties with
friends and relatives, we should not grudge the single person the
gadgetry that gets the housework done faster. If he or she can
indulge in occasional luxuries, there is a good case for seeing these
as the legitimate perquisites of being single, just as constant loyal
companionship at home is a legitimate perquisite of being married.

Most single people, too, do not have the alibi against materialism which is provided by being a parent. They cannot say that they are earning and spending for a better life for their children, but must frankly admit that they work for a better life for themselves.

The traditional role of wife, moreover, also involves psychological tasks such as helping to make decisions, rebuilding the ego after a setback, and generally lending a sympathetic ear. Those who live alone, as the majority of single people do, must rely on friends to provide this companionship, and maintaining friendships usually involves spending extra money on such things as good food and drink, transport, public entertainments and the telephone. Companionship is not a luxury but a necessity, and for the single person living alone such spending is a necessity also. One has to learn to disregard the traditional view that time and money spent in the home are morally better spent than time and money spent elsewhere, that (for example) it is more 'Christian' to buy a bottle of wine for a family dinner than to buy a round of drinks in a pub.

'Life wouldn't be so bad if it weren't for the times when you're supposed to be enjoying yourself', my brother once said to me in a pessimistic moment when we were both teenagers. Very true, for work at least provides a basic structure for life. When the holidays come round some single people find that complete freedom is a very mixed blessing. Christmas and other festivals are already notorious as the low points of the year for those who are vulnerable to loneliness, and the single person, even when not lonely, finds that they are celebrations of the family rather than the community. As for longer holidays away from home, single people who cannot travel with friends or relatives have the choice of joining a group of strangers or travelling alone. Both can be very enjoyable, but both have their drawbacks. Travelling alone means that one loses the satisfaction of sharing new experiences, and for some women, to be honest, it brings an element of anxiety. Women on their own are quite frequently subjected to bureaucratic rudeness and commercial crookery where a man or a couple would not be, and, even in Britain and much more overseas, are sometimes regarded with suspicion and even hostility. Being pestered by strange men, too, is an amusement where the fun quickly wears off, and being older or less attractive just means that one gets pestered by older and less attractive men. Joining a group, however, sometimes means going to the opposite extreme, perhaps finding that two-thirds or even more of the party are unattached women, and that the activities are as regimented, and the rules of conduct as petty, as if one were back at school.

There are, of course, group holidays organized especially for single people, and a study of these would make a book in itself, an interesting book too, which would reveal a great deal of the ambivalent attitudes of single people towards each other and their position in society. In my own experience, exaggerated romantic expectations had been raised in some of the women members of the party that could not possibly be satisfied, and some skilful leadership would have been needed to raise the level of mutual tolerance and co-operation needed to make the holiday a success. Holidays for the single are commonly very expensive, inconvenient as to time and place (often completely inaccessible without a car), and sometimes the advertising emphasizes the opportunities for sexual adventure to such a degree that they put off anyone who takes sexual relationships seriously, or prefers other forms of leisure activity.

Most advisers of the single woman urge her to make constructive use of her leisure, by spending it in study, or sports, or voluntary work, or church activities, usually saying that these pursuits will not only be rewarding in themselves but will also make her more interesting and attractive to men, and give her a chance to meet them. Unfortunately it seems to me that more often than not these benefits cannot all be obtained from the same activity, and some choice has to be made. Happy is she who joins a voluntary work group of eligible bachelors. What more usually happens is one evening working for a good cause, another studying at home, and a third out looking for the bachelors. Those who live alone may well expect to have to put more effort into their leisure lives than the married person, but it may not be possible to pursue all these worthy aims at the same time. Most single women appreciate the greater chances they have of complete relaxation, what Margaret Adams charmingly calls 'going to bed with David Copperfield', but some are driven by loneliness or the fear of it into taking on more leisure activities than they can really cope with.

I think this danger would be much reduced if the advisers were more honest about the use of leisure as a means of seeking the company of men. I would say that the means of meeting up with men that they suggest, such as evening classes or voluntary work, do not as a rule produce even a reasonable choice of possible husbands, let alone enough congenial men friends to provide masculine companionship until such time as one stops feeling the need for it (if ever!). Serious and worthwhile spare-time activities usually involve commitment to a group for a long period. The time thus spent may indeed be rewarding in other ways, but is virtually worthless if the real purpose in joining in was to find a man or men. To do this one has to take part in activities which involve large numbers and a high turnover, and be prepared to spend money on them. The best of both worlds is achieved by social clubs, but there are not nearly enough of these that seriously cater for people between thirty-five and sixty. It may seem trivial, but I wish that Christians would be more realistic about this use of leisure and treat it in a way that would encourage single women to be honest with themselves. Are single men given this kind of advice? (If so, they are obviously not following it.) Is it un-Christian for a woman to admit that she wants to meet men for their own sake, and not because she wants to get married? Must she pretend to have a burning interest in badminton or the Labour Party? Seeking new friends may involve a Christian woman in taking some risks, including moral risks, in choosing the places to spend her leisure and the company to be found there, but there is nothing un-Christian about this. It is better to follow the example of Jesus himself than of the majority of Christians who prefer to stay in 'respectable' surroundings.

Though independent in theory, in practice the single woman finds her leisure restricted by the attitudes of other people, and her problems in this area reflect the problems of her life as a whole in a particularly exasperating way. In our society where violence is on the increase, especially violence against women, the leisure of the single woman is threatened not only by real dangers, but even more so by the attitude that women should not seek to lead an independent life. Women who come to grief are therefore seen as in some sense deserving their fate, and all women are encouraged to be unadventurous and to rely on other people for leadership and security.

7 | *Family relationships*

When Susie was an auntie, an auntie Susie was.
Ice-creams all round, ice-creams all round. . . .
(Playground rhyme, c.1975).

Moving on from the single woman's life in her job and public leisure, the next two chapters will consider how the fact of being single affects her private life, particularly her relationships with four important categories of people: children, her own parents and other close relatives, married women friends and men.

In Christian literature, single women are not expected to become mothers by intention. In one of the earlier books, this is stated in terms of morality:

Deliberately seeking to bring an illegitimate child into the world is indefensible from both a social and a personal point of view.[1]

Single parents are, of course, mentioned in Christian literature, but only when motherhood is an established fact, when writers are concerned with a woman who *has* children and has lost her husband, or who *has* parted from the father of her child without marriage. Actual and potential motherhood are not discussed in the same context. Motherhood, even of single women, is treated as part of family life. Single women who *might* some day be single mothers are considered by other writers and treated as a completely different category of person. In Christian literature on single women the dominant note on motherhood is one of regret for what may never be, without consideration that for some single women it will be, or indeed already is.

Since then there have been appreciable changes in the social dimension of single motherhood. The invidious social distinctions that used to be made between the children of the ex-wife and the children of the unmarried mother are blurring as a result of the increase in numbers of the former with the increasing incidence of divorce. Many of today's illegitimate children are born of couples co-habiting without marriage, which means that they do not lack the care of their fathers, nor does illegitimacy necessarily mean that the child is being reared at the taxpayers' expense – as many legitimate children are. I do not wish to minimize in the least the economic difficulties of unmarried mothers, but only to point out that these hardships are no longer directly linked to the single status. This would throw into greater prominence the personal dimension of this question, which I take to be the ethics of a sexual relationship outside marriage, to be discussed at greater length later. Meanwhile, however, I think it is a pity that Christian writers on single women have passed over the subject so quickly. The close connection between marriage and motherhood in our society means that it is hardly appropriate to consider one without at the same time thinking about the other. There is nothing *natural* about our assumption that having a child means committing oneself for life to the child's father, or conversely that a marriage is incomplete and unsatisfactory if it does not produce children. These assumptions are two of the social factors that determine the condition of single women, and by thinking about them as such the single woman will be better able to assess her own personal situation.

One writer, Gini Andrews, suggests that a single woman who wants a child should adopt one. This is legally possible in Britain – and an advantage that single women have over single men – but does not often happen in practice. Better contraception, and the increasing number of unmarried mothers who choose to keep their children, have led to a shortage of children available for adoption, and a single woman is most unlikely to be allowed to adopt in preference to a married couple.

Generally, however, Christian writers assume that the single woman will remain childless for as long as she remains single, and they suggest ways in which the lack of a child may be compensated for in relationships with other people's children. Since I have never experienced my own childlessness as a personal deprivation, I do not know how far the roles of aunt, godmother, teacher, nurse and so on actually relieve the frustration of an unfulfilled desire for motherhood, but I do know that the social aspects of childlessness also affect women who do not have this desire.

It would perhaps be inaccurate to say that the Christian community over-values motherhood in the absolute sense, since one might say this was impossible. It is certainly possible to over-value it in the relative sense, however, by over-valuing it in relation to other possible achievements of women, and some Christians do this. This is very dangerous in the global sense, because, quite apart from the value of alternative ways of achievement, the future of the human race on this overcrowded planet demands that more women must reject motherhood, and it is also dangerous to the individual woman. Some Christians are guilty of helping to increase the numbers of unwanted and ill-treated children, and unhappy mothers, by a rigid and inhuman attitude towards contraception, abortion, homosexuality and even childlessness itself, and by continuing to convey to women that it is only by childbearing that God's creative power can work through their lives.

I have also come to resent the fact that single people who are not parents, teachers or educational administrators have so little say in the upbringing of the next generation, though they are taxed for the education of other people's children and will have to live with its results. The parent-child relationship, like all close relationships, is one of power as well as love, and those who are not parents, though they may love children, and enjoy being with them and helping to care for them, do not have much real influence over them. 'Ice creams all round' is fun but it is not the same as a real stake in the future. Child-rearing is now taken so seriously that parents are very reluctant to let anyone not professionally qualified share their responsibilities. Women such as myself will not only never pass on their genetic assets (such as they are!) but have no clear way to pass on whatever life may have taught them. A successful mother can teach her daughters about marriage and motherhood. Success in single life is not taught or learned so readily.

The Christian institution of godparenthood might perhaps be more used to remedy this. It is my impression that in former days single people were preferred as godparents. Perhaps it was hoped that a childless godparent would help the godchild materially as well as spiritually, by advancing him or her in a career, or leaving money in a will. It would be interesting to examine the non-religious aspects of godparenthood more closely, to find out whether the role could be updated to give more influence and status to the single person. Except for temporary roles such as bridesmaid, this is the only formal relationship for which a single person can be chosen. All others are the result of birth. This makes it important, and perhaps it could be made more so.

Being a child oneself when one is adult is never easy – advice on the tactful handling of in-laws and grandparents abounds in all literature on family life. When a daughter is adult but single, much depends on how the relationship has been managed during her adolescent years. Parents have to strike a difficult balance between urging their daughter to seek independence, including finding a husband in due course, and holding her back by restricting her relationships with men they think unsuitable, or diverting her to other activities such as study or housework. When they do not strike this balance very happily, the situation tends to get worse over time, as their real power over the daughter's behaviour diminishes and they have to resort to persuasion. Some parents nag their daughter day and night to get married and supply some grandchildren, others urge her to stay at home and look after them in their old age. (One woman told me her parents were doing both 'on alternate days'.) Yet even these extremes of behaviour do not usually arise from totally selfish motives; parents are as much victims as daughters are of the contradictions of women's lives in our society. The marriage arranged by the parents has virtually disappeared from Western society, which means that parents can do very little to help their daughter to marry, even if she wants to. Nor can they do very much to relieve loneliness, except by making her an honorary member of their own generation.

When parents grow old and dependent on their children, it is far too often the single daughter who ends up carrying the whole burden of looking after them. Longer life expectancy means that she is now more likely to be doing so when she herself is in late middle age, with health problems of her own. Over 300,000 single women in Britain are supporting parents on their earnings alone. Others have had to give up their jobs because the parent needs full-time care. The National Council for the Single Woman and her Dependants, which exists to protect the interests of such women, can furnish some appalling stories of poverty and social isolation, such as to make the choice of marriage on any terms seem preferable to the chance of drawing such a hand for one's declining years.

Even with the best will in the world, most single women are at some disadvantage when dealing with parents, married brothers and sisters and other close relatives. In our society marriage is the true coming of age ceremony, granting the right to a home of one's own, an adult sexual life, the right to express and act on opinions which differ from those of one's parents, the right to set other relationships and duties above those of the family one was born into. None of these can be counted upon with certainty by the unmarried, though naturally some parents are more liberal than others, and some daughters more rebellious. It is hard not to feel that one has disappointed one's family by remaining or becoming single, even if they never say so, and some do say so. Since they have a vested interest in marriage, it can be impossible to convince them that being single is best for you, even if it's true. If it isn't true, the feeling of being the Ugly Sister at the wedding, the Bad Fairy at the christening, can be very painful indeed. The conventional family visit or celebration nearly always involves the single woman in playing second fiddle to a married hostess, and to those who have domestic news to tell and children to show off. When family rows occur, the single woman usually finds herself arguing alone against two or more, and it is easy to give in when you know that you will otherwise have to face the bitter aftermath alone, or when the self-confidence of your opponents is built on more emotional satisfactions in the past week than you have had in a year.

For some single people, men as well as women, leading a single life has forced them to cut themselves off from their families, perhaps the only people who really care whether they live or die, because their families have become the spearhead of society's pressure to marry and be 'normal'. Even more frequently, the rituals of visiting and telling news are kept up, but real concerns and feelings are never mentioned, because the family cannot or will not offer support in leading a happy single life, as opposed to expressing sympathy or concern about what they feel is an undesirable situation. Unless parents and family understand that not all women have the same ambitions and capabilities, and that a career, friendships, solitude and so on can be alternatives, not merely substitutes, for a husband and children, their support for a single woman may be generously given and valuable up to a point, but never complete. On the other hand, some families do provide support, constantly and ungrudgingly, for long years after the time when they might reasonably have expected a husband to take over.

8 | *Friends*

> I said that I could venture to guess from her face she had never been married. I told her it was from her cheerful disengaged countenance (Sir Walter Scott, *The Heart of Midlothian*, Introduction).

Friendships between single and married women rest on an insecure foundation. By the time that most women marry, in their early twenties, at least five years will have passed during which they have been expected to find men more interesting than one another. There may be several reasons for this, but one of them is social pressure to find a husband. When most women do find one, they have become used to making friendships with other women take second place. Marriage is expected to change a woman's whole way of life, and often does, particularly if she now has more, or less, money to live on, or adopts her husband's friends and interests in place of her own. Sometimes the cutting off of everything and everyone who had a part in her single life can seem quite deliberate, and curiously enough I have found this happens more often with women who marry late than women who marry early. Even when continued friendship is desired on both sides, practical difficulties arise. The single woman's home may be unsuitable for entertaining a family, or the wife may be too tired or too busy or too short of cash to invite friends to her home. Marriage can also mean moving to be near a husband's job, or migrating from a city centre to the outer suburbs. The conventions of formal visiting make it difficult to see a wife apart from her husband, and if she has young children one can spend hours in her company without ever getting any adult conversation, which can be very frustrating indeed.

A wedding is supposed to be a joyful occasion, when people look forward to seeing the couple grow and change together. Inevitably this leaves a bitter taste for those who liked them as they were. But past family relationships, no matter how drab or conflict-ridden, will be kept up to a minimal extent. For their

single friends the loss may be complete. A few really close friendships will survive, but the minor ones will be expendable. This
matters more than appears at first sight. We all need to be loved,
but I think Christians underestimate the importance of being
liked, of having less intimate relationships with people who appreciate your good points but will not be too badly hurt by your
defects. The loss of less intimate friends when they marry does
diminish the quality of life as a whole. For a while at least, moreover, married women, with their strong common interests of
home and children, are better placed than single women for
making new friends. While her contemporaries are busy with
young families, the older single woman finds that she is spending
most of her leisure with people who are either much younger than
herself, or, less often, much older. There are advantages to be
gained from this fact, of course, but in this rapidly-changing
world it can be rather difficult to form close friendships with
people in a different age-group.

Family life involves family loyalty, and if this conflicts with
other loyalties, it may be right that the family should generally
come first. I have been really shocked, however, by the ready
acceptance of the view that conflict of loyalties is inevitable, and
that single people must just fit in as best they can, as in this
opinion from a single woman writer:

> One thing every single person has to beware of is trying to
> share the lives of married friends ... their lives no longer in-
> clude you on the old terms ... Do not make any mistake about
> it; single people have to lead a different social life from that of
> their married friends; to assume otherwise is to ask for trouble.
> The way to reconcile yourself to this is to accept it as a fact,
> just as an alien in a foreign country accepts the fact of being a
> foreigner, or a person with a physical disability has to accept
> the difference between himself and other people.[1]

Should the rights of single people be so unequal that they must
compare themselves to exiles and cripples?

When the single and married friends are of different sexes,
another obstacle is placed between them, that of sexual jealousy.
I must make it clear that I do not in any way defend adultery, and
accept that a single woman must not only avoid stealing a husband's affections, but also behave in such a way that suspicion and
scandal, however unfounded, do not arise. I also accept this in

cases where the marriage is unhappy – as it usually is, since a happy marriage is not so likely to be affected by anything the single woman may do. In cases where the marriage is legally at an end, or no longer exists in any sense but the legal one, one's attitude must depend on one's acceptance and interpretation of Christian teaching on marriage and divorce, which is outside the scope of this book.

Like all other problems facing single women, however, the temptation to adultery has social as well as personal components. The convention that a woman should desire a man who is richer, cleverer, more ambitious, more successful and older than herself, means that some clever and successful and otherwise very moral single women find that there are not enough of this kind of man to go round, and decide that a part share is better than none or an 'inferior' one. This also goes to show, however, that the criteria used to judge a marriage can be positively unhelpful when used to guide single life. When I stopped looking at men from the point of view of a would-be wife, I discovered that many of the sound, reliable, successful men were really very pompous and boring, and the misfits began to seem less sinister or pathetic and more interesting. Several of the earlier writers on single women warn their readers against friendship with homosexual men, or men with serious character defects such as extravagance or being over-fond of drink. Taking this advice too literally would greatly impoverish the lives of single women; good friendships are possible with men with whom marriage would be a disaster.

As the rights of family over friendship have been overstated, so have the rights of marriage in particular. For example:

> All the men with whom I worked were married. That meant I was rightfully cut off from real fellowship with them. Finally . . . I said another big 'yes' to the Lord . . . 'if you want me to be forever barred from a conversation with a man about anything but work and weather, all right'.[2]

Just how much is this real fellowship worth if it can be brought to an end by marriage? Surely it is possible to avoid adultery without creating emotional apartheid between married and single?

Granted, not all moralists are as strict; this author is writing of small isolated groups on the mission field. In more normal circumstances most single women associate with large numbers of married men, which probably in most cases decreases, rather than increases, temptation. Though adultery remains a potential trap for single women, this is to me a less depressing thought than recognizing so many men who proudly claim that they have never looked at another woman since they married. Often this is all too obviously true; they have not made the slightest effort to show any interest in or understanding of their women acquaintances, colleagues, employees or even relatives. Some men are such robots in their public life that one can only hope that they turn into human beings when they get home.

Conversely, the single woman must not be prevented by moral scruples from showing friendliness to married men, even if this means admitting to herself that she likes the husband better than his wife. Now that many married women have jobs, the problem of finding that one has much more in common with the husband is tending to diminish, and a joint friendship with both partners is easier to establish. It is also the case that some married people feel that their single friends are neglecting *them*, and no doubt this complaint is sometimes well founded.

Among single people too, over-valuation of marriage can stifle and distort what might otherwise be valuable friendships. (Sometimes this over-valuation takes the perverse form of seeking to avoid it at all costs.) Friendships between single women and single men take place against a background of social expectations that the main purpose of such friendships is to provide a good choice of marriage partner. This not only leads men and women to look for ulterior motives in each other, but also means that if their friendship is not in some way related to marriage, other people see it as incomplete, unresolved and uninteresting. If a single woman talks about a close friendship with a man, she finds it hard to gain any interest or sympathy unless she allows her hearers to fictionalize it in one of two ways – as leading to wedding bells and general rejoicing, or else to some dramatic form of trouble such as a broken heart or an unwanted pregnancy. If neither of these endings is in fact on the cards, it is difficult to make other people attach any significance to the friendship at all, and both parties may even be accused of wasting their own and each other's time with it.

Moreover, when a single woman talks about men friends, she does not have the moral protection afforded by the married woman's happy ending to the story. The wife has preferred one man above others, the single woman's tale has no hero, only a heroine. Her story is that of one woman and many men, and this gives it a morally ambiguous tone, a touch of the Sunday papers, even when the relationships were blameless in fact.

Similarly, some wives will admit that they made most of the running in their courtships, but imply that they were prompted by overwhelming love of the man they eventually won. The convention that the man should take the initiative does to some extent protect him from blame and ridicule if the woman rejects him. Women are supposed to proceed by roundabout ways, by flattery and attention-seeking which many women and some men find trivial, tedious and humiliating. For the woman to take the initiative is only justified when it is successful. An overture which fails brings not only rejection by the man, which can be bad enough, but also social penalties for 'unwomanly' behaviour. The loosening of formal conventions has increased the ambiguities and mystifications surrounding relationships between unmarried people, and more than ever there is a need for honesty about one's own feelings and understanding of the feelings of others. The scales are still heavily weighted in favour of those who are determined to marry, or content with short-term and superficial affairs. Those who want friendships that last long enough to develop naturally, but not inevitably into marriage, find that what they want is hard to come by, and even when such friendship comes it seems quite pointless to other people.

A single person may come to learn that quality counts for more than quantity, and that having few close relationships, or none that lasts for very long, does not mean that those relationships were not worth having. But being single can mean that all your relationships are superficial, or embittered by the knowledge that you are needing someone who doesn't need you. In all personal relationships, not only sexual relationships, the single person's love has no rights. Other people may want their company, appreciate their good qualities, offer help when needed, but none of these things can be demanded. And they must learn this after at least two decades of learning the opposite, of expecting to establish loving relationships in family life, where family members have the right to be dependent on each other emotionally as well as economically. Making and keeping enough friends to satisfy the need for love and companionship throughout life takes more, not less, qualities of character than finding a marriage partner and having children. Those who think of single people as 'immature' should remember that they are obliged to learn a kind of love that cannot be backed up by social sanctions. It approaches, perhaps, to the ideal of Christian love which gives without demanding a return.

The Christian, however, can claim family love in the Family of God, the church. What place does the single woman find there?

9 | *The family of God and the nuclear family*

Patriarch and holy prophet,
  Who prepared the way of Christ,
King, apostle, saint, confessor,
  Martyr and evangelist,
Saintly maiden, godly matron,
  Widows who have watched to prayer,
Joined in holy concert, singing
  To the Lord of all, are there
       (Bishop C. Wordsworth, 1862).

Christian life has come to be far too closely identified with the life of the nuclear family. Even the most casual observer of the Christian scene must notice that many institutions exist for the guidance and fellowship of children, teenagers, wives, mothers and (sometimes) men, but for the adult single woman there is often nothing but roles requiring special talents such as teaching in Sunday school or singing in the choir. Where there are activities for women in general, they very often take place at times when the single woman is at work, or have such a domestic flavour that she feels out of place. Much pastoral energy is devoted to the direction of Christian marriage and parenthood, in sermons, discussion groups, published literature and so on, while the single person is seen as one who can be called upon to help in Christian ministry without ever being on its receiving end, unless so unhappy as to need individual counselling. Single people can join in general social gatherings, Bible study, church government and so on, but they do not have the same chances that married people do to study their way of life, help each other cope with its problems, and make the most of its advantages.

The Christian community has learned over the ages to be cautious about too close involvement with human institutions, but the family has been made an exception to this. I have heard from the pulpit that the family is God's invention and that Jesus always upheld its values. Both these statements are highly debatable. What kind of family did God invent? The Old Testament family that allowed polygamy, child murder (Jephthah's daughter), incest (Lot's daughters) and selling a wife to a heathen ruler for political gain (Abraham)? Or the New Testament family, founded on slavery and the subjection of women? God may have invented the ingredients, but the recipes have been devised by man. 'Family' is an umbrella term covering a wide variety of institutions which attempt to satisfy certain human needs. God has not revealed to us what an ideal family would be like, and even if he had, we should not be justified in rejecting all other ways of life.

Whatever God may have done to found the family, or does to help us care for one another within its social framework, he certainly did not invent our present situation, which is well described by Rosemary Haughton:

> ... societies such as ours that pay lip-service at least to the value of loving personal relationships can also use this very fact to distract attention – and love – from the need for, or even the possibility of love in the wider political sphere ... Those, in fact, who attack the 'bourgeois' family ideal on the grounds that it deforms the individual's capacity for relationships are attacking it on its strongest side. More cogent is the charge that it confines love to the 'private' domain, and so, in effect, to a privileged class of people ...[1]

It is no coincidence that the nuclear family is the only life-style supported by social sanctions such as the law. The family provides an outlet for values and emotions which might otherwise hinder the smooth running of our society. Friendship in general, and other ways of living in community, are not so sanctioned because they have the potential of growing into larger groups and even mass movements which could disrupt the present class and economic system. Our economy, for example, depends very much on high consumer spending by small households, and the inheritance of property and class status depends on establishing the legitimacy of children. Capitalist society and the nuclear family are mutually supportive institutions. This must not be taken to mean that either should be done away with, but merely that both are human institutions which should not be held above criticism or immune from change. We should never accept any human institution as the one ideal way for Christians to live, and there will always be people for whom family life is inappropriate. The 'wider political sphere' includes not only the public areas of social life where expediency rules because altruism has been relegated to the home, but also the private life of those people outside the nuclear family.

If family life were really as fundamental to Christianity as some Christians assert, it is indeed strange that Jesus never said so. F. R. Barry writes:

> Nothing matters more to a free people, nothing matters more to the Church, than this nursery of faith and character, sanctified by the life of the home at Nazareth.[2]

We know nothing of the home at Nazareth except that it produced an eldest son whose first recorded action was to run away from his parents and cause them much anxiety (Luke 2.41–52), who showed indifference to his relatives all his life (Matt. 12.46–50, Mark 6.4), warned his followers that discipleship would split their families apart (Matt. 10.34–38, Luke 9.57–62), and did not make provision for his mother's old age until nearly too late (John 19.26–27).

Among more conservative Christians the image of the family is often used to justify authoritarianism and sentimentality, restricting development of democracy in church government, and over-emphasizing the fatherhood of God to such a degree that many Christians never see the need to think for themselves as adults. Religious life is called upon to sustain family life ('The family that prays together stays together') as if it were the family, not the prayer, that was the chief good. This can only encourage those who promote religion primarily as a means of 'being good', or even those non-Christians who trade on our heritage of 'Christian family life' in efforts to control the behaviour of young people, or outlaw certain forms of sexual behaviour, or censor the arts, without at the same time extending the benefits of the Christian faith, which is much more than a cheap means to moral righteousness or emotional security.

The single person may also be disturbed by the controversies of modern theology, which have created confusion between the great text 'God is love' (I John 4.9) and its converse: Love is God. Love in human relationships is one way in which we experience God, but it is not the only way, and some Christians seem to go so far as to say that God *exists* only in human relationships:

If there be a God – and we have to admit that Jesus thought so – we can find him only in our neighbour, when our neighbour has become a friend.[3]

If we make love the condition for experiencing God, we act very differently from Jesus, who never asked those that he made whole whether they loved God, or him, or each other, but whether they had *faith*. Nor shall we be made whole by our love, not even if we achieve the love by which Jesus forgave his tormentors, let alone by the natural human affections found within the family. It is a fact that there are plenty of people around who have not known human love since they lay in their mothers' arms, and some not even then. This is a terrible condition, but it does not mean that for such people God does not exist. Single people are, of course, not necessarily loveless, but many are in a position to know that human love cannot ever be taken for granted, either in other people or themselves.

Efforts to encourage the growth of love among Christians, though often devoted to the building up of internal Christian fellowship within a church, more frequently take the form of either urging those already bound by close emotional ties to improve the quality of those relationships, or on the other hand, of promoting charitable work to help strangers in need. The 'neighbour' level, where affection may be impossible and charity inappropriate, is often neglected, but it is on this level that many single people have to live in relation to the rest of their communities and each other. It is very important indeed that those who have 'failed' to achieve 'normal' family relationships should not be made to feel that they are thereby cut off from God or less than full members of the Christian community.

As far as single women are concerned, the worst effect of over-emphasis on family life is that the single Christian life has been given very little serious thought since the Reformation. Protestant Christianity has almost completely rejected the monastic way of life, and it is apparently proving unsatisfactory for Roman Catholics also, since the number of women in religious orders has declined dramatically over the last twenty years (see M. Bernstein's book, *Nuns*). This may not be a matter for regret, but comparison of the situation of the single woman in secular life with that of the nun shows that not all the advantages are with the former. Ideally, the nun enters a lifelong career of organized Christian service – at the price, of course, of her rights over property, sexuality and self-determination. Other Christian single women take no vows, are free to earn money and worldly status, to associate with men and to prepare for marriage. The nun, however, is never without someone to turn to when she is old, sick, poor, lonely or perplexed, and she can hold to the belief that her sacrifices are not only acceptable to God but also respected (if not understood) by the rest of her society. Her single status is finally and publicly defined, entered upon with solemn preparation and ritual, and this must surely be a great support even to those who have not a shred of genuine vocation.

It seems that in some quarters there is an awareness of the absence of a theological framework for single life today, but no serious attempt appears to have been made to remedy this. The following is quoted from the Anglican Commission report on *Marriage, Divorce and the Church*:[4]

> There are those who, for a wide variety of reasons, remain unmarried; and some do so voluntarily. In the Christian tradition there have always been men and women who have renounced the right to marriage in order to give themselves wholly to the service of the kingdom of God ... In Christian thought and experience there are close parallels between the way of dedicated single life and the way of marriage. In both cases it is affirmed that man's whole life can be consecrated to God in faithfulness and love. In both the value of permanent human relationships is underlined; for though the great majority of unmarried people do not take vows, the vows of religious life, where these are undertaken, also involve lifelong commitments. The religious community, which these vows safeguard, provides much of the continuity, reliability, and challenge, which are such an essential part of marriage. Without taking vows many other unmarried people find in the permanence of their dedication to their work, particularly work with people, a similar element of continuity and reality ... The unmarried Christian finds, in his or her relationships with married friends and their families, a complementarity of role and function which seems to have a God-given quality about it. Although apparently opposed, the two ways in Christ support and illuminate one another.

I find it remarkable that this report, admitting that only a very small minority of single people live in religious communities, has so little to offer those who do not, let alone those who did not choose to be single, or have been married and lost their partners. The emphasis on permanent human relationships is particularly distressing, since it is in this area that single people are most vulnerable to frustration and guilt, and since there are so many powerful social forces at work that hinder the formation of any permanent relationships outside the nuclear family. Nor has enough allowance been made for the fact that singleness is generally regarded as a highly undesirable state, and the permanently single or formerly married person is often the object of misplaced pity, scorn and suspicion. Single life is here being represented as still closely associated with heroism, self-sacrifice, the vocational professions and virginity. There have recently been loud and justifiable complaints from married Roman Catholics about the dire results of having their church government and family life controlled by celibate people, and there has not, so far as I know, been any corresponding benefit to those who are single for reasons other than religious vocation. It could well be, too, that single Protestants are equally hampered in their religious life by the fact that nearly all people in authority in their churches are married.

The family of the church and the single Christian

I am become as it were a monster unto many (Ps. 71.7).

The lack of any theological foundation for single Christian life today is at least partly responsible, I think, for the misguided attitudes to the single person that are displayed in Christian pastoral teaching. Using the family as a model for the church as a whole may distort our way of thinking about the single way of life in general. Using the family as a model for individual congregations, however, is even more likely to produce an image of the single person as outcast and victim, to be restored like a prodigal son or daughter to the blessings of 'normal family life'. If this process of trying to make a local church more like a family is then extended to actually using the human families of its members as the basis of all its communal life, there is a strong probability that single individuals will not only appear as outsiders but actually become so.

Obviously, it would help nobody to return to the days when most Christian single women were heroic freaks who went into convents and missions and so on, and the rest were just freaks. I wonder, though, if it is not unhelpful to insist, as most Christians appear to, that single women are just like other women and want exactly the same things out of life that their married sisters do. I know quite a few single women who cannot stand what passes for 'normal family life' for more than about three days at a time. It is right to recognize that single people are not all eccentric and 'odd', but not all want to be incorporated into the majority's life-style. Some have developed life-styles of their own.

Christian literature on family life quite frequently mentions the situation of Christians who have no family of their own, while non-Christian literature on the same subject seldom acknowledges their existence. One can also find some quite perceptive comments about the needs of single people, and a willingness to be sensitive to their feelings. Why, then, should I be so dissatisfied with what

I have read in this context, and with my own experience of the relationships between the single and the married Christian? It is not just that the subject is considered entirely from the married person's point of view, for that is only to be expected. The basic problem is that the two states are very seldom indeed seen as alternatives. The contrast is always between fulfilment on the one hand and deprivation on the other. When any practical suggestions are made as to how the married person should behave towards the single person, one can see very clearly that even voluntary single-ness is seen as a social problem.

In his book *Pastoral Ministration*, for example, P. E. Johnson refers to single people as 'homeless', which is certainly patroniz-ing, and to my mind borders on unintentional insult to the many single people who are justifiably proud of their homes and have made them places of great security and cheerfulness. Christian writers addressing single women directly, most of whom are them-selves single, encourage their readers to acquire a pleasant home and use it for the practice of hospitality. Johnson also recommends Christian families to take single women as lodgers, to give them the benefits of family life in exchange for the 'social graces and spiritual gifts' which many single women possess, and which can 'enrich family living'. It does not occur to him that these gifts might have been given to enrich single living. Moreover, though taking her into a family home might benefit a single woman in terms of relieving loneliness or poverty, it makes her into a depen-dant and social inferior. To be on equal terms she would have to become part owner of the house, not just a lodger or even a tenant. However kind the welcome, there is always a difference between the home you enter by permission and the home you enter as of right.

Other writers do recognize that single people do more for the community than just help out with family life (by acting as tem-porary substitute parents, for example), that they are sometimes exploited by those who assume that they have unlimited spare time and energy, and that they sometimes resent sympathy. Anne Townsend, for example, in *Families without Pretending*, quotes with understanding a bachelor friend who complained of being treated as an 'adult orphan' and a 'stray dog' to be given 'a meal, a place on the rug by the fire, and a few anxious there-theres in the ear'. Yet the same bachelor is quoted as saying 'If I am on my own for any length of time, all sorts of maggots spring to life inside. It's a vicious descending circle of frustration and despair.' We hear nothing of single people for whom solitude is a blessing and whose single life is helping them to become more truly themselves.

Mrs Townsend is also typical in seeing the single person's deprivation of family life as a potential threat to the life of *her* family. She warns that a single woman may suffer if over-exposed to the sight of caresses between husband and wife, and that if she appears to be too much attracted to the husband the relationship should be tactfully brought to an end. There are no warnings that the wife may become envious of the single woman's freedom, nor any recognition that the single woman's relationships with men may be, for her, equally satisfying. She does not caution the wife against embarrassing the single woman by signs of unfounded jealousy – this happens more often than one might think, and it is very difficult to give reassurance, since there is no polite way of telling her that one would not take him as a gift. And in this and in most other contexts, it is always assumed that the initiative lies with the family, that the single person needs them and not the other way round, that they will direct the course of the friendship.

Christian literature also tends to hark back to the extended family of apostolic times, and to use it for a model for church life today, as described, for example, by Rosemary Haughton:

> . . . a real community whose heart was a definite biological family, though the family did not constitute the real household . . . In Christian households of the apostolic period the 'extra' people are not really 'extra' but are all part of the same household, which includes 'the family'. All, equally, belong . . .[1]

Whatever may have been their condition in former times, there is no doubt that today those outside the nuclear family *will* be 'extra' to the 'heart of the community' if we see the creation of such a community in terms of drawing all members of a church into family life, and by appointing the heads of families to be the chief sources of Christian comfort, as the same writer suggests a few pages later:

> . . . the couple as the heart of a new Christian community, creating a home where the weak and sorrowful will be welcomed and helped.

There is another point of view to be considered, and that is that the gospel view of the family of God is a family which will one day include the whole of the human race, and meanwhile all

Christians are brothers and sisters, whether married or single, adults or children. Community life can equally well be created by getting everyone out of their homes and treating them as equal individuals on neutral territory. At the very least there should be some consideration of the possibility that single people may be able to share some benefits of their way of life with the married.

Married people, either as individuals or as people in authority in a church, cannot do anything to help a single woman gain or keep self-respect so long as they persist in thinking that the life of the nuclear family is the only road to emotional health and leading a morally upright life. Christian literature contains many very biased portrayals of 'alternatives to the family', implying that they are huddles of dirty, needle-scarred layabouts, or else some kind of human battery-farm. In fact communities of single people, in addition to the monastic orders, have existed for centuries, and are now on the increase as the monastic orders decline. A whole denomination was once formed from communities of single Christians, the Shakers of America, who lived very much as rural hippies do today, except for a fanatical insistence on celibacy. In spite of this they lasted for well over a century, which suggests that they fulfilled a real need. (Their other beliefs included equality of men and women in church government, and worship of God as female as well as male. In this they were a long way ahead of their time, and it would be interesting to consider how these beliefs could be adopted by unmarried communities today.) In society in general, and to some extent in the Christian community also, alternative ways of living together are attracting serious study and gaining some degree of acceptance.

Companionship in community life can be made available to single people without obliging them to take vows or abandon their jobs. But if continuity is to be maintained for more than a few years, the members will be faced with situations which challenge their commitment, whether they are free, for example, to take up a better job in another town. There might also be conflicts between the rights of the community and the rights of the family, if members wanted to marry, or had to take over the care of elderly parents. Another possibility of community is the 'singles church', but this can be set up only in a large city where there are enough single people to support it. Small informal groups can be very valuable indeed; I shall always remember with gratitude the members of a singles group at Harvard Epworth Methodist

Church in Cambridge, Massachusetts, whose modest programme of Sunday lunches and occasional excursions made a very real difference to my life in the USA some years ago. Such a group, however, depends very much on there being a few reliable and creative individuals to keep it together, and yet prevent it from degenerating into a closed clique. There are also problems involved in catering for single people of different ages and levels of education.

Some people will not unreasonably object, moreover, that any move to bring single people out from the rest of the community is counter-productive, and will make for nothing but an unhealthy self-consciousness. The number of single adults in any one congregation is usually small, and special activities for them may make them feel uncomfortably conspicuous. If they join forces with single people from other congregations, it would be all too easy to give the impression that single people are being thrown together in an attempt to pair them all off. The chief aim must always be to improve single life, and for this fellowship is essential, but not enough in itself. The common factor of singleness, moreover, will not in itself create fellowship, and the formation of a group identity will have obstacles in its way. Any new group identity of a minority brings with it the possibility of trouble, and in the case of the single, latent hostility may be stirred up between single men and single women, between heterosexual and homosexual, between the permanently single and the formerly married, and between those who want to marry and those who do not. If single people begin to proclaim the value of their way of life, some of their married fellow-Christians may feel that their way of life is being disparaged. The Harvard Epworth group had chosen the colourless and inaccurate name of 'Young Adults'. I heard later of a similar group in Texas that called itself the 'Venture Single-Aires', an interesting contrast, I think, between self-images of the single, and though it may appear a little brash, I think the latter is the one to aim for.

One can anticipate that many single people will be very reluctant to discuss single life publicly, even in a singles-only group, or commit themselves even for a short time to membership of a singles community. For some individuals, and in some social environments, to declare openly that single-ness is part of one's identity will require as much courage as it does for the homosexual to 'come out'. (Some single people would indeed be

obliged to do both at once.) Many single people do not feel the
need for help in living single life, and (a common characteristic of
socially disadvantaged groups) those who are successful in it do
not always feel obliged to help those who are not. Some think,
indeed, that one of the secrets of living single life successfully is
to maintain mental and emotional independence by *not* discussing
it with other people. Unless some initiative is taken by single
people themselves, however, and the problems and advantages of
single life discussed more openly than they usually are at present,
then single people must continue to depend on whatever help they
may get from the married majority, and if they do this their status
as 'problem people' is unlikely to change.

Loneliness

A want of companionship maintained in my soul the
cravings of a most deadly famine (Charlotte Brontë, *Villette*).

Perhaps it is not quite fair to say that single life is never seen as
anything but a problem. It may be that those who describe it in
such terms have had much experience of dealing with single people
who are admittedly unhappy. British people are notoriously tolerant of eccentric individuals, and a single woman who claims to be
contented though husbandless may be genuinely believed – while
all goes well with her. When things are not going well with her,
she will find that although other people may be tolerant and sympathetic towards her as a person, they are not tolerant towards her
way of life. Very few will look for the causes of her unhappiness
beyond the fact that she is single, and the range of personal
deprivations that she may be supposed to be suffering as a result.

I have tried to show, however, that while the effect of personal
deprivation varies with the individual personality, the social disadvantages experienced by single women in their upbringing,
employment, leisure, personal relationships and life in the church
all have a common factor. They tend to make the single woman
feel that she is 'abnormal', and to isolate her from the common
interests and activities of those around her, not merely in her own
perceptions but in reality. Many single women are able to forgo
some or all of the benefits of marriage without regret, but very
few women do not feel the need for true companionship, if only
on occasions. Many solitary people are not lonely, and many others
have proved able to withstand the effects of loneliness to a remarkable degree, and it should be emphasized that being single does not
inevitably mean being lonely. I think it is true, however, that in
our society single people are exposed to what might be called a
high occupational risk of becoming lonely, and also that their
chances of obtaining effective help if they do become lonely are
reduced by social attitudes to single life.

No one who has experienced real loneliness, even for a short period, will need convincing that it is a destructive condition. We are well accustomed to using it as a punishment: 'I won't speak to you again', 'Go to your room until you can behave properly', 'sending to Coventry', 'solitary confinement' and so on – yet many people are enduring in their daily lives a degree of loneliness that would be thought excessively cruel if they were in jail. The loneliness of old age, so common as to be almost acceptable in our society, can start before you're thirty. Young people too go missing and are never heard of again, young people kill themselves because they have no one to turn to for help, young people die alone and lie unburied for weeks. Young people too take to drink and drugs and overwork and other self-destructive behaviour, or spend all their leisure time in a lethargy, because of loneliness. I doubt if there is any defect of the human personality that loneliness is not likely to make worse, and it stifles good qualities that have to be practised in relationship with other people if they are to become a habit. For many lonely people all the Christian teaching about the importance of mutual love and personal relationships is nothing but the order to make bricks without straw.

I have already mentioned that one reason why most women wish to marry is that they fear that single life will eventually turn them into cranks. Some sociologists, however, such as Phyllis Chesler and Jessie Bernard[1] state with convincing evidence that mental illness is in fact less common in single than in married women. What one can infer from this, however, depends on one's definition of mental illness. It is perhaps not very surprising that phobias, hysterical outbursts and psychosomatic disorders should be less common in women who depend entirely on their own earnings for a living. Loneliness, however, though it causes as much suffering as mental illness, and carries something of the same social stigma, is not in itself the sign of an unhealthy personality; rather the reverse. It is not 'sick' or 'abnormal' to suffer from the 'want of companionship', any more than it is sick or abnormal to suffer from hunger while being kept short of food. And although there is a subjective element in loneliness (as there is in hunger for that matter) – that is, some people need or think they need more companionship than others, the regular contact provided by a job does not always prevent loneliness. A person can be severely undernourished even when not actually starving. Just as undernourishment lowers resistance to disease, so loneliness lowers resistance to real mental illness and deterioration of character. Acute loneliness can destroy the ability and even the motivation to relate to other people at all.

Loneliness is not only destructive, it is dangerous. A really lonely person will do anything for companionship, no matter how tedious, futile, irresponsible or degrading it may be. This causes lonely single people, who generally have fairly free use of their leisure time and money, to become very vulnerable to exploitation, not only in such matters as working too much overtime or being 'company' at short notice at the whim of other people, but also by bogus religions, extremist political groups, and every kind of racket designed to take advantage of those who feel personally inadequate or have some kind of chip on their shoulder.

There seems to be a natural human tendency to blame the individual victim when society has no answer to the problem. In ancient times, those whose crops failed had not propitiated the right gods; in more recent days those who could not live on their wages were stigmatized as feckless and greedy. Nowadays if you're lonely it's because you don't deserve any friends. Loneliness, however, does in fact have social as well as personal causes. Isolation is a matter of environment as well as character, and is increased or decreased by the neighbourhood one lives in and the organization of one's work. A lonely person is not necessarily disagreeable, or stupid, or crazy, or even shy, and since it is quite commonly assumed that the older single person is all or any of these merely by reason of being single, stereotyped thinking about singleness and about loneliness is mutually reinforcing and leads to even greater misunderstanding of the single person's needs.

Single people are particularly vulnerable to the effects of another even more widespread but more subtle fallacy: that lonely people will cease to be lonely if they can be thrown together. This makes about as much sense as removing the doctors and nurses from a hospital and telling the patients to get on and cure one another. Loneliness *is* like a disease in that once past a certain point, lonely people in association cannot do much to help each other and can easily make each other worse. Obviously, the most sinister effects of this fallacy show up in 'pairing off' the single. Many a disastrous affair or marriage has resulted from acute loneliness in both partners, sometimes helped on by ill-considered matchmaking by other people. I am even more concerned about the traditional teaching that the cure for loneliness is to befriend another lonely person, with its underlying hint that perhaps all that is wrong with you is a touch of self-pity. It may be true that some people lose hope more easily than others, but associating with someone even more wretched does not necessarily help them to recover it. It is bad enough to have to cope with one's own loneliness. To take on someone else's as well can be the last straw; and many single people realize that their absence of family responsibilities makes them more, not less, vulnerable to a lonely person who demands more of them than they want to give.

The same fallacy also affects people in larger groups. A group of any size over about thirty people is certain to include a few individuals who are just about hanging on to the edge of normal social behaviour, but can very easily be pushed over it into despair or hostility by some chance word or misunderstanding. As a new-comer to a London church many years ago, I was invited by an older single woman to call on her for a chat any time I wanted company. When I did so about a week later, she shouted at me from a window to go away, and it was some time before I re-covered enough to realize that she had not recognized me and was even more lonely and mistrustful than I was myself. Incidents such as this have convinced me that those who wish to combat loneliness must try to make sure that acutely lonely people do not exploit those who are vulnerable to loneliness, and also that the true cure for loneliness, when it is discovered, will involve the association of lonely people with those who are *not* lonely.

For the same reasons, I have doubts about the long-term effects of therapy directly aimed at the cure of loneliness, such as encounter groups and the like, even when organized on a Christian basis. Stirring up powerful emotions without providing a regular outlet for them in future, and causing people to strip themselves of all dignity and restraint without reckoning how they are going to feel when they are alone again next morning, seems to me every bit as immoral as seducing them sexually might be. On the other hand, some more traditional forms of social gathering actually involve very little real interaction between those who take part. It is very frustrating for a lonely person to be at close quarters with other people, yet denied the opportunity to try to get to know them. Perhaps the trouble with both kinds of group is that fellowship cannot be forced into existence, yet neither does it always develop out of mere acquaintanceship.

This could be one reason why voluntary service is so often recommended to lonely people, that in theory it will bring people together with a common aim to work for. There is a danger, however, that it will only increase their sense of aimlessness by deepening their confusion about what it is they really want out of life. The boundless faith placed in it by some Christian counsellors seems to me exaggerated:

> In whatever field of human life it is undertaken, the giving out of devoted service, even of the simplest and most humble kind, will inevitably lead to some real relief from loneliness and to the creation of new and enduring friendships.[2]

Unfortunately this is not true. Happiness is sometimes a byproduct of good works, but in some cases the lonely woman ends up feeling yet more guilty and inadequate at not responding to treatment, or yet more bitter and resentful at being recruited for the voluntary workforce just because she has admitted to being discontented with her lot. A lonely woman does not primarily need to feel useful to other people, but to feel that her happiness is important to them. Happiness is a precious human resource that should be fostered as carefully as intelligence or goodwill, and there is no need to think that a happier person will not be as good a Christian. Misery may cause a woman to turn to God but will not keep her there, and it is worth remembering that an unhappy Christian is an even worse witness for Christianity than an immoral one.

Loss of self-respect is the greatest obstacle to enjoying solitude, and also to establishing friendship, and no plan of action alone will restore self-respect when it has been lost through lack of confidence in one's whole way of life. Having chosen to live in independence should not mean that the single woman must feel a failure if she cannot endure her loneliness or cope unaided with everything life throws in her path. God did not intend any of us to be as independent as that. Neither did he intend that an unhappy single woman must abandon her belief that single life can be right for her, any more than the unhappy wife must write off either her own marriage in particular or marriage in general.

Failure to recognize the social factors that isolate the single person causes far too many counsellors, even professionals, to ascribe the unhappiness of the single woman to personal failings or regrets. They convey the message that society will not change and she had better adapt herself to the majority view. For the single woman, however, the only way in which she can effectively do this is to get married, whereas the unhappy wife can at least adapt herself to known individuals who may reward her for doing so. In the case of Christians, unhappiness can all too easily be attributed to spiritual emptiness or rebellion against God's will. If the single woman cannot accept this, there is nothing for her to fall back on but to assume that she has mistaken her vocation and 'ought' to be married – which could be a very dangerous notion – or to accept the non-Christian belief that singleness must inevitably be less fulfilling than marriage because it is 'unnatural'.

Loneliness is an unnatural state, but in most people's minds the alleged unnaturalness of single life does not refer to loneliness but much more specifically to sexual deprivation. Any single woman who says that she wants to get out more and meet new people will find that at least half her hearers will interpret this as meaning that she wants to find a husband, but more than ninety per cent will interpret it as meaning that she has had enough of sleeping on her own. Though I feel that this use of loneliness as a euphemism for sexual deprivation does not tally with the actual experience of single people, I do nevertheless regard the vexed question of sex outside marriage as extremely important in consideration of the single state. It is the only area of life where traditional Christian teaching enjoins totally different conduct on single and married people, and nowadays it is practically never discussed from the point of view of the single Christian as an adult.

12 | *Sexual relationships outside marriage: moral aspects*

> Girls! I will let down the side if I get a chance,
> And I will sell the pass for a couple of pence.
> (Stevie Smith, *Collected Poems*).[1]

The Christian community, not before time, has recently abandoned the long-held doctrine that all sexual activity is sinful in itself, and recognizes once more the scriptural view of human sexuality as part of God's loving energy which sustains his creation, and as one of his gifts to human beings for their use and enjoyment. Interpretation of this rediscovered belief, however, still varies very widely indeed when applied to the day-to-day moral lives of individual Christians. It seems to me that the aspect of sexual morality which has been least affected by this change is the prohibition of sexual intercourse outside marriage. Attitudes to those who go against the prohibition are now, it is true, much more lenient than they were a generation ago, but their actions still go by the hard old names of fornication, promiscuity and 'living in sin'. Love and affection between single people are permitted and even encouraged, but it appears to be still taken for granted that for these to lead to a fully physical relationship is no part of a Christian life.

Some very conservative Christians are now finding it possible to incorporate the new attitude to sexuality in their teaching on marriage and family life, but even the most forward-looking Christians become confused and wary when applying it to the sexual lives of the unmarried. It is now easy to discover what makes a Christian marriage right, and the place of sexuality within it is readily acknowledged, but it is surprisingly difficult to find a clear and up-to-date statement as to why non-marital sexual relationships, hereinafter referred to as 'affairs', are wrong. (The term 'affairs' is used in preference to the more modern 'pre-marital intercourse' in order to get away from the idea that all single people will eventually marry, and to exclude intercourse without consent. It refers to relationships of any duration for which both partners have moral responsibility.)

After very thorough consideration of the subject, it became clear to me that the continuing doubt and confusion in Christian moral teaching is the result of the persistence of two traditional arguments, one moral and the other theological, which will now be discussed in turn. This distinction between morality and theology is somewhat artificial and should not be taken to imply that God is not concerned with moral issues in the relationships between people, nor that theology is confined to actions attributed directly to God. For a Christian it might be more appropriate to think of these two arguments as considerations of this kind of relationship first in the light of what our knowledge of God tells us about human relationships in general, and then secondly about what it tells us about sexual relationships in particular. In practice, however, the moral arguments draw heavily on non-theological ideas (such as the findings of medicine and psychology), and are upheld by many people who do not believe in God at all. For the second kind of argument a belief in God is essential and he is considered to be far more directly involved in the human relationships under consideration.

Briefly, the moral argument states that sexual intercourse outside marriage invariably results in someone getting hurt, and the theological argument rests on the idea that God instituted marriage as the ideal, if not the only, means of expressing physical sexuality. Both these traditional theories have one basic idea in common: that non-marital sexual relationships are wrong – or at least suspect or imperfect or immature – purely and simply *because they are not marriage*.

Moral arguments against the undertaking of affairs state, rightly, that it is wrong to use one's sexual capacities to exploit another person, that is, in such a way that you are profiting at their expense. It is also wrong, less obviously, to behave in such a way that another person is tempted to exploit you. Whether exploitation actually happens, however, in any particular relationship, must depend not only on the people involved, but also on their social environment. Paul's description of fornication as 'joining Christ's body to a harlot' (I Cor. 6.15) makes sense on the moral level – leaving aside the theological meaning for the moment – when one remembers that in his day all women except harlots were the property of another man, a husband or father or other legal guardian, and so illicit intercourse was an infringement of *his* rights, besides leaving the woman without support for herself or her children. Today, though single women have legal rights over their own bodies, and a much larger measure of economic independence, society is still structured in such a way that affairs provide opportunities for exploitation. It is no longer so obvious, however, exactly what exploitation takes place and who is to blame for it.

Until very recently the person who was most likely to suffer exploitation in an affair was the unwanted child who very commonly resulted from it. Today, conception is in theory avoidable (and not all illegitimate children are unwanted) – but no contraceptive is as yet as effective as abstinence. There are still also wide possibilities that the affair may injure other people: family members, friends, colleagues, anyone who may be made to feel betrayed, ashamed, guilty, neglected, jealous or envious, or given an example that leads them into trouble.

Curiously enough, however, these possibilities of wronging third parties attract far less attention from moralists than the risk that the couple involved will injure each other or themselves. Perhaps this is because arguments based on wrong done to outsiders can only be conditional, and the couple might reasonably feel free to go ahead once they had done all they could, by using contraception, for example, to prevent harm to other people. Consideration of danger to the couple themselves makes it easier to establish an absolute argument, by backing it up with some statement about human nature in general, such as:

> Since the sexual life of the female consists of baby and home, as well as intercourse with the man, she is only getting one-third of her sexual life ... The result is that she suffers from attacks of inexplicable panic, headaches, palpitations, 'bands' around the forehead, fears of insanity and a host of physical discomforts which she does not understand.[2]

The use of 'female' in opposition to 'man' neatly enhances the basic idea that women are creatures of animal instinct, and it is interesting that the ailments of the fornicating female have also been ascribed at other times in history to the practice of masturbation or prolonged virginity. (Today, they sound more like the symptoms of an overstressed mother.)

I quote this piece of by no means unique nonsense to show why I am suspicious of any moral argument, of whatever date, that is based on universal theories about sexuality, whether these are explicitly stated or taken for granted. The following, more recently written, for example, reads at first sight quite convincingly:

> Because it does not satisfy man's real needs or fulfil the demands of his nature as man – Christians would add, man as God has created him – therefore fornication is always morally wrong.[3]

The preceding sentence, however, shows that the underlying theory has not changed:

> The male orgasm, it should be remembered, is a single act, bringing instant relief. For the woman, it is the beginning of a cycle, ending in birth, lactation and motherhood, which she is precluded from fulfilling.

This is a very narrow and biased view of female sexual nature – and of male sexual nature for that matter. It is not difficult to see the problems involved in basing today's moral teaching on the legal and social systems of biblical times, but it is equally important to see the danger of basing it on supposedly absolute theories of human sexual nature that will seem totally absurd in less than twenty years' time.

The following words, though taken from a novel, ring far more true to real experience:

> What upset me most was not having to give up my little boy, nor bearing him, nor being shamed, but being lied to and sponged off all that time. I thought I'd found somebody who cared about me, but it was all lies and self-deceit.[4]

This girl was hurt in the way that all human beings can be hurt, by the betrayal of love and trust, and never mind the experts on the 'sex life of the female'. It can happen in any close relationship, between parents and children, brothers and sisters, friends, colleagues and comrades. Is it inevitably more shattering, or more likely to happen, in a sexual relationship? Most people seem to think so, but if so, why?

Perhaps it is because nearly all moralists on this subject are obviously concerned entirely with relationships between young people, including those too young to marry, and they are not unreasonably afraid that young people may rush into situations they are not mature enough to cope with. This should remind us, however, that it is not only the heedless young who are specially vulnerable to emotional damage, but also lonely disillusioned older people, who need to give love as well as to receive it, and are perhaps more in need of affection and companionship than of intercourse itself. One should not assume, however, that all older single people are vulnerable in this way, just as it is rather a pity that so many Christian moralists assume that all young people are heedless.

Concentration on young people probably also accounts for the somewhat disproportionate emphasis given to statements that an affair will spoil one's chances of a happy marriage later on. This is not limited to obvious dangers such as venereal disease, but includes more vague psychological risks, such as a greater readiness to be jealous or unfaithful. This case is founded on some reality, but it cannot be made the foundation of an absolute prohibition; indeed strictly speaking it is not a moral rule at all, since it is based on the fear of consequences. Real experience also tells us that many women now happily married did not turn up at their weddings as virgins. Moreover, most women are obliged, long before they can think of sex and marriage in terms of a real individual man for whom they can have real individual feelings, to think of them as part of their life's career, in which 'success' is essential. When a woman abstains from choice, or to safeguard a real relationship, one can call her chaste; when she allows consideration of marriage as an event that may not happen for many years, perhaps never, to dominate all her existing relationships, it is harder to give her that name. Christians are commanded to be prudent, but not at the cost of being unloving.

This is only the most obvious way in which our ideas about marriage are constantly used as the criteria for judging the morality of all other forms of sexual behaviour. By labelling them degrading, or at best inferior, we give the would-be seducer of either sex a powerful incentive to be dishonest about his or her motives and intentions. Perhaps even unconsciously, every relationship is disguised as a preliminary or an approximation to marriage, and the 'victims' may well collaborate in the pretence to avoid admitting, even to themselves, that they are settling for less than total commitment. Some of the blame for this must surely rest at the door of a society in which celibacy is almost as much disparaged as other forms of non-marital sexual activity, and in which any woman can so easily be made to feel inadequate and deprived if she does not achieve marriage and parenthood, or at the very least find some non-relative of the other sex who can be induced to say (if only once in a lifetime) 'I love you.'

I 3 | *The way forward: extending the moral frontier*

> An ethic that sets out a list of rules about bidden and
> forbidden actions tends to cut us off precisely from what we
> ought to be doing, which is to listen to others to discover
> what we ought to do (Michael Keeling, *What is Right?*).[1]

The very existence of marriage shows that a difference between
sexual and other close relationships is upheld by custom and
morality. We have come to expect, if not to tolerate, different
kinds of behaviour in them. Physical intimacy is expected to open
the door to brutality and insincerity as well as to tenderness and
understanding. We seem on the surface, perhaps, to expect people
to treat their sexual partners better than their ordinary friends,
but no one is greatly surprised, it does not seem unnatural, if they
end up treating them far worse.

It is only in marriage, however, that this tendency is countered
by socially sanctioned morality. Even when the marriage partners
do not really fully intend to be faithful, they live under a code
whose existence, if not its validity, is not questioned, and this at
least provides some guidelines for behaviour. The partners in an
affair find it harder to know how they should act, harder to know
what they may justifiably expect from each other, harder to resist
the temptation to neglect their partner when he or she is in
trouble, or to desert him or her for someone more attractive.
Where partners do not owe each other the total commitment of
marriage, the result is that they are not quite sure what they do
owe each other. It can give them the idea that they do not owe
each other even the basic rights of human beings: to be told the
truth, to be consulted in decisions that affect their future, to make
their own decisions free from emotional browbeating, to have
their bodies and their feelings handled with respect. By going outside the moral structure governing sexual relationships, which in
practice is applied only in marriage, they may feel free to disregard
all moral considerations and act according to the feelings of the
moment. This may happen in a marriage too; the partners think

that marriage sets the final seal of approval on their relationship and from then on they can do as they please.

It is easy to account for the difference between sexual and other partnerships by psychological factors, showing how closely love and hatred are related, and how the sexual behaviour of adults is affected by childhood experience. Any consideration of the subject is incomplete, however, if it does not take into account the structure of society as a whole, and the way this affects all relationships, sexual and other, between men and women. Men are accustomed to assume authority over women in all aspects of life, and since this imbalance of power can only be maintained by distorting the nature of both sexes to some degree, even the best of individual relationships bears some shadow of the false notions of masculinity and femininity that we are all obliged to learn. Obedience to the simplest of moral rules, do as you would be done by, is something of which a good many men are not capable where women are concerned, because they cannot imagine how they would feel as members of the subordinate sex. Love alone certainly does not justify a relationship while a man can quite sincerely love a woman and still exploit her every day of the week, expecting her to live primarily for his care and comfort, because they have both been taught that this is natural and right.

'Taught' must sound like an exaggeration. I think, however, that as the traditional arguments against non-marital sexual relationships gradually lose their validity, and as we learn to judge such relationships on their own merits and not by reference to marriage, it will become apparent that men and women are in fact educated to exploit or at least manipulate each other's feelings in order to get the best for themselves out of their sexual relationships. I am not thinking only of pornography, which teaches men to exploit women, or of the kind of romantic literature which gives women a false and mawkish image of men. Even those who obtain 'sex education' from authorized sources such as the school curriculum are not learning to treat each other as human beings. They are still taught that members of the 'opposite' sex (a significant term) are more alien and more alluring than they actually are. They learn that it is 'natural' for men to dominate women and for women to try to 'get round' men, and that a woman's personal worth depends chiefly on her relationship with a man. Chivalry is certainly not dead, the strong are taught not to exploit the weak, but there is not much questioning about who is going to be strong and who is going to be weak. The cruder forms of non-chivalrous behaviour, such as shouting obscenities at women in the street, are frowned on, but it is still perfectly acceptable for a man to believe that women are funny (in both senses) creatures, and that nothing they do or say need be taken seriously. Anyone who taught young people to relate to other races in this way would soon be in real trouble. In sexual relationships, where the differences between men and women naturally assume a great deal of importance, it is all the more essential that neither should lose sight of their common humanity.

On the other hand, judging all sexual relationships by the same criteria as marriage, and by traditional thinking about the nature of men and women in general, also leads to false perception of exploitation where none exists in reality. The charge often brought against partners in an affair, that they are 'undermining marriage', is often true in the sense that they are rejecting marriage as it has been presented to them. There are strong social pressures on single people, particularly women, to seek out a marriage partner who is like them in age, class, race, education and general cultural background. Those who find themselves involved with someone who is different in these respects, or who do not want to live together all the time, or have children, or to be dependent on someone else for money or housekeeping, or to associate with each other's friends and family, or to set the relationship above their job or some other interest, may opt for an affair rather than marriage. Not all women who did not get a wedding ceremony were hot-bloodedly raped or cold-bloodedly seduced. Some really preferred to begin the relationship with a minimum of fuss and not after a long tiring day of standing around in a white dress being scrutinized by their relatives. Some honestly believe that the danger of exploitation is less in an affair than in marriage. They cannot commit themselves to a social contract that seems to them so unequal, especially if they would have to seal it by religious vows. A sexual relationship may lack any or all of the ingredients that are thought essential for marriage and still be much more than a cheap means to physical pleasure.

The greatest difference between an affair and a marriage, however, is that marriage is intended to be permanent and an affair is not, or at least is not guaranteed as such. Many people tacitly accept that an affair may benefit both partners while it lasts, but foresee that the good will be undone when it comes to an end.

(This contradicts another commonly held belief, that a long affair is 'better' than a short one, even in cases where a long-term affair is racked with conflict and a short one is friendly and cheerful.) We accept that broken marriages, broken engagements and un-requited love cause sorrow and humiliation, but in the case of affairs it is thought inevitable that the end will bring guilt and bitterness as well. If it does not, the relationship was 'mean-ingless' or the couple were 'hardened against normal feelings'. The torments of jealousy are anticipated, particularly for the woman:

> Few women can face the idea of sharing their man with someone else – now, a year from now, or ever.[2]

The assumptions behind such statements are very illuminating: temporary possession means that the man is 'theirs' for life, but only if the relationship included physical intercourse. The loss of a man's love and companionship may be heartbreaking, but why are matters worse than in a broken 'romance' that did not include intercourse? I suspect that a large part of this kind of bitterness is due to feeling cheated of some mythical right to a secure and exclusive sexual relationship, and to terror at the thought of hav-ing to survive on one's own, perhaps for good. Is it always the man who tires of the relationship first and moves on to another partner? Must the woman feel guilty and degraded if she too looks forward to finding another man? Perhaps both are affected by the fact that our society is a network of couples, and neither may be able to count on much sympathy or companionship in the com-munity when the couple relationship breaks down. Ask any widow or unwilling divorcee if social disadvantage does not exacerbate the pain of personal loss. Yet this does not put women off getting married.

Moral arguments must inevitably be influenced by the social climate of a particular time and place. We should do well to base our judgments on values that we can believe to be eternal, such as justice, truth and compassion, and we must also take into account the developments of the foreseeable future, such as the invention of a hundred-per-cent reliable contraceptive, or the increasing economic and psychological independence of women. It is time that Christians gave up the idea that a sexual relationship outside marriage is exploitative by its very nature, and set out to find what makes some such relationships more exploitative than others. This does not mean that we should extend the code that governs marriage to govern other sexual relationships as well. The two kinds of relationship are not the same, and so their rights and duties may well be different too.

I am not, of course, recommending that there should be a new list of 'rules about bidden and forbidden actions'. I am suggesting that the frontier of Christian ethical thinking should be extended to include sexual relationships other than marriage, that they should be discussed, not only in the abstract, or in private counselling, but openly, so that more Christians should become aware of their potentialities for good as well as bad, and so as to reduce the mental gap between those who think of sex entirely in terms of marriage and family, and those who think of it in other contexts. Those who, metaphorically speaking, see the ideal sex life as regular and nourishing square meals often do not understand how anyone can endure, let alone enjoy, the feast-and-famine existence of the single person. Some single people, however, find it better than outright starvation, and others actually prefer it. Those who insist on regular square meals do not make good explorers and had better stick to well-mapped territory. The territory of sexual relationships outside marriage is still a wilderness, but today it is beginning to attract the pioneers as well as the bandits. Until Christians have drawn some kind of moral chart of it, instead of just marking it 'here be dragons', they are not in a position to judge its inhabitants, and they are not in a position to make convincing statements about it on the theological plane either.

In the long run, all statements about the effects of such relationships are incapable of proof. To say that they cause jealousy is more convincing than to say that they cause headaches and palpitations, but only relatively so. Restating the case in terms of theology, the traditional argument asserts that God does not bless such relationships. They end in guilt and bitterness because they have offended him.

| *Sexual relationships outside marriage: theological aspects*

> As a father has compassion on his children, so has the Lord compassion on all who fear him. For he knows how we were made, he knows full well that we are dust (Ps. 103. 13–14).

Theological arguments against sexual relationships outside marriage fall into two fairly distinct strands, which might be labelled the chiefly intellectual and social, and the chiefly emotional and individual. On the intellectual side, marriage is systematically described as a sacramental state of self-giving, the expression not only of sexual and romantic attraction, but of a true Christian charity which desires only the good of the other. It is essential that this relationship should be exclusive and permanent. There can be no turning back and starting again with a different partner, except when one partner has died, or divorce has taken place – not allowed except under certain stringent rules which vary from one church to another. Any sexual relationship less complete in its commitment than this is imperfect from the beginning and therefore sinful. The other school of thought places less emphasis on relationships between people, and more on the relationship of love and obedience between the individual Christian and God, established by Jesus at a terrible cost in suffering. To go against his will by illicit sexual acts is to betray this relationship, and as it were to degrade Jesus by our degradation of ourselves, this being the meaning of I Cor. 6.15, already quoted in chapter 12.

The first kind of argument is often extremely difficult to understand, let alone accept, being frequently expressed in theological gobbledygook such as:

> ... the act itself is misused because it is made to express less than it fully symbolizes and so is prevented from effecting what it naturally signifies.[1]

The supporting arguments are based chiefly on theories about the theological nature of sex in the abstract. Sex does not exist in the abstract, however, but only in the sexual natures of individual people, and so shows enormous variation in its nature. Sexual morality is not concerned with sex as a natural phenomenon, but with sex as a social phenomenon, subject to change as the structure of society changes over time. (It is not so very long since, for example, that 'normal' women were supposed not to feel sexual desire at all.) Just as interpretation of scientifically observed phenomena can change radically within a generation, so also can the interpretation of the (surprisingly few) references to sexuality in the Bible. Sexual morality must also concern itself with homosexual relationships. Most theological arguments based on 'nature' either ignore these or dismiss them as 'against nature', which makes me suspect that such arguments are only marginally relevant even in the case of heterosexual relationships.

Speculations about the nature of sex usually include comparison of the sexual behaviour of humans with that of animals, with an attempt to show that only in marriage is sexual activity truly human, otherwise it is pleasure without responsibility, comparable with animal behaviour. F. R. Barry uses the analogy of the social ceremony and cultural ritual that surround a meal, as contrasted to the mere feeding of animals. But man cannot escape responsibility. If he misuses sexuality he is not an animal but a sinful human being. Physical pleasure is not in itself degrading (if it were, Christians would be forbidden many harmless amusements such as dancing and swimming). Above all, this is the masculine side of the story; few women experience sexual relationships as nothing but physical pleasure.

Now that sexual activity is not considered sinful in itself, those who forbid it outside marriage are forced to use terms that are more positive than in the past. This leads them to carry their praise of the benefits of Christian marriage to a somewhat ridiculous level. It is not only the young, attractive, prosperous and well-adjusted single person who takes an interest in this subject, and this approach breeds cynicism in those who know that they are difficult to live with, and may expect to encounter many difficulties in marriage – should they ever get the chance to try it. This is also strongly at variance with much Christian teaching on marriage itself. The marriage service, for example, is very realistic about the need for God's grace in overcoming difficulties. Over-emphasis on the sacramental nature of intercourse itself can have a similar effect. We do not try to turn every meal into a Holy Communion;

and while both human beings and animals engage in sexual activity, it is only human beings who laugh at themselves while doing so. The reverse side of this idealization of marriage is an overstatement of the dangers of non-marital relationships which sometimes, frankly, amounts to theological scaremongering:

> The sexual union is a *total* commitment – as mystics used to say, in some ways it prefigures the union with God, demanding a self-surrender only less complete than the surrender to him. And where it is less than total it is hardly worth having – a momentary pleasure, a permanent loneliness.[2]

I feel sure that the majority of ordinary married Christians would be more moderate both in their exaltation of marriage and in their disparagement of other kinds of sexual relationship.

This kind of argument is usually combined with assertions of the need to maintain the family as the basis of the Christian community and of society as a whole. It was probably easier for single people to accept their own duty in maintaining the family, in the days when there were recognized alternative institutions for themselves. Now that traditional teaching on vocations for single people has dropped out of sight, the single person's role in the maintenance of church and society goes unacknowledged. One can therefore more easily respect the more personal approach to this issue, since this does at least recognize that affairs can be more than the result of childish hedonism. Those who are aware of the transitory nature of all human relationships, as many single people are, have a strong incentive to take very seriously their relationship with God, which on his side will never change or fail. Like any other relationship, however, it takes time to develop to the point where it will withstand powerful emotional impulses, and there are obstacles to this development where sexual behaviour is concerned. I doubt, for one thing, whether most young women will have time to build it up before they reach the age of susceptibility to sexual impulses. The long period between puberty and marriageable age means that a girl's education in chastity must begin long before she can marry, and also long before she is really capable of understanding the Christian teaching on the alternative vocation of celibacy. In any case she will probably never hear the latter, since Christian sex education, like other sex education, is nowadays a preparation for marriage, and the alternative, which involves permanent sexual abstinence, tends to get glossed over.

We also tend to forget that temptations against chastity include
the temptation to remain chaste for the wrong reasons – such as
fear and pride – and very young girls are as easily led into prudish-
ness as into promiscuity. Assuming responsibility for one's own
sexual life is also delayed by over-identification of Christian life
with the life of the family. The confusion of God's authority with
that of the parents, natural enough in childhood, tends to be prolonged into adolescence, and it is in sexual matters that adolescents
most resent parental interference.

Gini Andrews notes that even adult women experience difficulty
in entrusting this area of their lives to God. Most women feel a
healthy reluctance to be too communicative with their human
fathers about their sexual lives, and this may well be carried over
into their thinking about God. We are often encouraged to draw
too close a parallel between human fatherhood and the fatherhood
of God. She herself demonstrates this when speaking of women's
emotional relationships with men:

> He wants to take your heart and shield it; He wants to keep it
> from breaking ... He knows our vulnerability in this arena
> where women have been losing battles for centuries ... God
> loves you too deeply to want to see you hurt.[3]

We will indeed go on losing battles for as long as we take refuge
in pietism rather than fight them. If, as I believe, the basic cause of
this vulnerability is the legitimized exploitation of both sexes by
one another, combined with the social subordination of women to
men, then it must be God's will that some women at least should
try to change the situation. Some will no doubt get their hearts
broken in the process, and some will face loss of their 'purity' as
well. A human father might be content that women should go on
being exploited so long as his daughter remains unscathed, but
ought we to think of God in this way?

It is quite a different matter for an individual woman to decide
that her personal relationship of obedience to God requires her to
be celibate, either temporarily or permanently. But for every single
woman to make God into the guardian of her chastity by dedicat-
ing only this aspect of life to him, with the idea that it is abstinence
that distinguishes the Christian single woman from the wife or the
unbeliever, and is therefore the outward sign of her relationship
with God, seems to me to be asking for trouble. Everyone knows
that to make a fetish of sexual purity only feeds the temptations

that one is trying to combat. If marriage is still a possibility, or single life has been entered on for reasons other than a total vocation, I am not sure that we have the right to expect God to be quite so closely involved in what is, after all, a matter for this world only. The one thing that Jesus is recorded as saying plainly about sexual relationships is that even in marriage they are not eternal (Matt. 22.30).

To make a personal relationship with God the foundation of sexual abstinence means that one must be sure beyond all doubt that he has set his face against all forms of sexual relationship other than marriage, and even more important, one must know why. I am not the first to point out that the ethical teaching of Christianity is far from systematic. For example, we believe that God has taught us to reverence human life, yet we are still in perpetual debate over the moral issues involved in war, capital punishment, euthanasia, abortion and suicide. In the same way, we are sure that God is offended by exploitative sexual relationships, but it is now debatable that a sexual relationship must be exploitative just because it is not marriage. Nothing in the gospel suggests that Jesus regarded abstinence as a badge of faith. He was heavily censured for associating with sexual outcasts, and the story of the woman taken in adultery (John 7.53–58) shows that he knew the sinner shared her guilt with the society she lived in. He neither condemned nor forgave the woman at Jacob's Well (John 4.8–30), though I think he did drop her a hint that her way of life would never fully satisfy her. He spoke of fornication as sin, but there is nothing to indicate that he was not referring to relationships which would certainly have been exploitative in the social context of his time.

If non-marital sexual relationships are not always and inevitably wrong on moral grounds alone, it becomes impossible to maintain the traditional teaching on theological grounds alone. A solely theological ban would mean that God's decree was not based on moral values but on a decision that it must be marriage or nothing. Theology and morality cannot be separated in this way if one believes in a God who commands us to love our neighbour. I for one find it impossible to believe that God's commandments are arbitrary. Much of the gospel is devoted to showing that while God is righteous he is also generous, and not only to those who deserve it. We cannot be sure that he will never bless certain acts or certain categories of people; he has overthrown too many of our taboos. I submit that he is not outraged by certain acts just because they are sexual, or just because they take place outside the traditional moral system. His anger is kindled not against the breakers of rules, but against those who 'overlook the weightier demands of the law: justice, mercy and good faith' (Matt. 23.23).

15 | *The way forward: a new theology of sexual relationships in single life*

> Wherever the most transient relationship has, as it may have, an element of true tenderness and mutual giving and receiving, it has in it something of good (*Towards a Quaker View of Sex*).[1]

In this chapter, I will try to collect a few thoughts which may point the way forward to a theology of chastity more appropriate to the single person.

Firstly, any new teaching on this subject must set itself further away from being merely a side-issue in teaching on marriage. Since many now single will eventually marry, the theology of marriage is not to be altogether discounted, but I am sure that most single Christians, not only those whose chances of marriage are low, would benefit considerably from having their sexual lives considered theologically as they actually are now, without continual reference to possible marriage in the future. Secondly, we need to focus more clearly on the fact that sexual relationships are relationships, that they involve more than one person. Traditional teaching shows a constant tendency to drift away from this reality, usually towards theories about human sexual nature in general, and towards the place of marriage in society and the church, asking 'What will happen to us all if single people are not celibate?' On the other hand, in teaching aimed more specifically at single people, the emphasis shifts to the solitary individual struggling with temptation, with attendant dangers of sliding into immature and inwardlooking personal piety, saying 'What will become of you if you are not celibate?' This reflects very clearly the stereotype of single life as either a preparatory stage for marriage, or a dumping ground for a small minority of subhuman or superhuman people. What is needed is for single people to ask each other *first*, 'What will become of the two of us if . . . ?'

For a relationship to be free from mutual exploitation and not directly contrary to God's will is only a beginning. The making and interpreting of moral and theological rules will never know

an end, but for those whose relationship has been blessed by God
the rules seem irrelevant anyway. Such a relationship cannot be
blueprinted in advance, or even described very accurately after
the event; it can only be experienced. Ultimately, one must turn
from theory to real life, and learn to trust one's own conscience.

The Bible, read as a whole, and the experience of Christian life
now and in past ages, provide a very general model for human
relationships of any kind. We learn that as the relationship between God and humankind is one of love, trust, faithfulness and
fulfilment, God intends our relationships with each other to be
similar. Love and trust bring out the potentialities for good in
both partners, so that the personality of each is not absorbed but
fulfilled, and this working towards a better self has effects not only
on the two people concerned but on others who associate with
them.

Learning from experience is not new, even on this issue. Traditional theology once held that any act of sexual intercourse, in any
circumstances, created a spiritual bond that was unbreakable while
both partners lived. If this bond was forged in an illicit relationship, both suffered spiritual damage that would prevent them from
making a true Christian marriage, or (presumably) from living a
truly Christian life in celibacy. Even while it persisted, this belief
was seldom acted upon. No one asked the bride at the church door
if she was a virgin, nor was she turned away when known not to
be. In the case of celibates, men and women who led unchaste
lives before hearing the call of God were sometimes afterwards
revered as saints, and only a minority of the religious orders refused admission to those who were not physically virgins. Today,
it can be openly admitted that both Christian and non-Christian
people, married and celibate, show the signs of God's blessing on
their sexual lives, even when they have had previous sexual
experience outside marriage.

This might be held to imply, however, that the previous sexual
relationships had not themselves been blessed, but that the past
had been wiped out by repentance and God's forgiveness, before
his blessing could be asked on the future. Marriage includes an
explicit promise to 'forsake all other' – it is perhaps a pity that
short of monastic vows the single person has no such opportunity
of publicly retrieving a lost reputation. There are reasons, however, for thinking that repentance of this kind did not necessarily

involve condemning one's past actions, even when it involved an intention of acting differently in the future.

Many Christian writers make a very crude contrast of marriage with 'casual sex' or 'promiscuity', implying that those who are not lifelong monogamists have no regard for their partners at all. Many draw a very rigid distinction between Christian love and erotic attraction, expecting to find both present in a marriage, but only the latter in an affair. Helmut Thielicke, for example, says that most affairs are undertaken as 'satisfaction of libido', and that both partners fall under 'a physiologically induced illusion that there are deeper affections or even some personal elements in the relationships. The libido is such that it generates such wish-images.'[2] In real life, however, distinguishing between love, liking and lust is very much more difficult than in theory, and even when they can be distinguished they appear and disappear and reappear with bewildering speed. Our faith is founded on the belief that love is more than an illusion founded on physiology, and therefore when love is present, even in a weak, misdirected or temporary form, it must be acknowledged as good. If 'satisfaction of libido' means that two people expect their affair to make them happier, the chances are that for a time at least it probably will, and this may make them kinder and more unselfish, not only to each other. If people are to be blamed when they cause injury to themselves and each other by an affair, it is only right they should also get the credit for good actions done under the influence.

Thielicke also likens an affair to trying to quench a thirst with salt water, but I think he is confusing quality with quantity. It might well be more like trying to quench a thirst with a teaspoonful when you really need a couple of pints, but even a fleeting opportunity to give and receive affection and physical pleasure can be very precious to those who have gone without it for too long. Such a relationship could better be compared to a mountain path that does not lead to the summit. Even those who did not get very high, or finished up no higher than when they started, may still feel that they have benefited from the climb. Love can only be learned by practice, not by study or observing other people, and the capacity to love can be increased, or decreased, by any relationship.

Any close relationship, sexual or otherwise, is bound to contain elements of both good and bad, but few are so very bad that one wishes they had never happened at all. We owe God an account of all that we do, but we also owe something to each other. To repent of engaging in a relationship just because it was not wholly good seems a kind of excommunication of the other person involved, which would be justified only in the extreme cases where the whole relationship was evil. If someone gives you a handful of pound notes and you find that only one of them is genuine, you are still being ungrateful as well as foolish if you throw the whole lot on the fire.

To repent of a relationship just because it included physical intercourse is even more illogical. It places an enormous and quite disproportionate emphasis on the loss of virginity, and no one has ever made it clear just when this happens in the anatomical sense, let alone the theological. The same physical action can mean many different things to different people. Most moralists discount 'technical virginity', but they still assume that a woman is not fully conscious of herself as a sexual being until she has intercourse, that is, that the status of full womanhood can only be conferred on her by a man, and that once this has happened she will lose the ability to lead a celibate life later on. The ancient definition of virginity as being a state of the mind rather than of the body[3] fits in better with the actual experience of women, and with Jesus' saying that even our thoughts are morally significant (see Matthew 5.27–28).

Single people need a theology of chastity that distinguishes more clearly between sex as a bond between people, and sex as bringing about bondage of the individual to his or her own sexuality. There is nothing supernatural in the desire of a woman to cling to her man in a man-dominated world, and I doubt whether physical instinct accounts for it either, while society exerts such pressure on women to be dependent on men for economic security and social status for themselves and their children. A man can escape dependence on one particular woman, but can still become dependent on sexual activity for its own sake. This dependence is far more easily disguised as something spiritual, and has caused men to make far too much of the need to struggle against their 'lower instincts', either personifying these in women or trying to 'protect' women from them. Sexuality is seen as a dangerous external force unleashed by women, which makes men lose their 'normal self-control'. Slavery to sexuality also exists in women, sometimes as the delusions of romanticism ('happily ever after') or as a hardboiled attitude to sex as the key to 'success' in life. Both sexes can be addicted to physical sexuality by the habit of masturbation.

Slavery to sexuality can, and does, exist even in those who have never experienced intercourse, let alone marriage. The converse of this, however, is that single people, even when not celibate, have potential ability to use their sexuality for good purposes as well as bad. We know, again from experience, that the capacity for having fulfilling relationships does not suddenly come into being over-night, or in isolation from other relationships. Christian teaching on marriage recognizes that sexual relationships are part of a process. They exist between people who have learned to love and trust and commit themselves to many relationships, with parents, friends, neighbours and so on, not only in sexual relationships. Single people need to be part of this process too, and insistence on celibacy at all costs can only hinder it. Social as well as psycho-logical factors mean that many of the close relationships of single people must be with each other, and if these relationships can be made more fulfilling, more expressive of the best in both partners, by physical intercourse, then they need that too. If such a relation-ship can be made more fulfilling by marriage, then they need *that* too, but for some single people fulfilment of their true selves will never be found in marriage.

All this is compatible with retaining the ideals of Christian mar-riage, and even with retaining marriage as an ideal sexual relation-ship, so long as it is recognized that marriage and non-marital sexual relationships are quite different in quality as well as in duration of commitment. The total commitment of Christian marriage is indeed a different kind of commitment from that found in other relationships, such as that of friend to friend, or teacher to pupil, or collaborators in some project or other. The crux of the traditional teaching is that where the body has been totally committed in intercourse, this must be accompanied by the total personal commitment of marriage; any other form of commitment is wrong.

If this teaching is rejected, it does not make so very much dif-ference whether the commitment of marriage is impossible, or merely being refused. What is left, and what does matter above all, is that both partners should be sure that such commitments that have been made will be honoured. God will not ask, as human judges do: were you married and if not why not, but rather: did you treat each other as you would be done by? Within the limitations that you both accepted, did you do your best for each other?

Those for whom the ideals of marriage will never be more than ideals need a morality not designed for teenagers, and a theology in which their expressions of love are not labelled sinful or immature or perverted or a waste of time when they cross some ill-defined physical boundary. They need a theology in which the sexual life of the single person, celibate or not, is recognized as something on which God's blessing may be asked, and deserving of the support of the Christian community.

> ... it may well be a case of the spirit being willing, but the
> flesh being not simply weak, but designed to work in the
> opposite direction (Margaret Evening, *Who Walk Alone*).

There is one respect in which Christian writers on the condition of
single women recognize the effect of the social environment, and
that is in their condemnation of the 'permissive society'. They
argue that being surrounded by sexual 'freedom' in other people,
the woman who is short of sexual experience can more easily be
seduced or blackmailed into a sexual relationship which she does
not really need. Quite true, but this also has other implications.

Though one can indeed find evidence that sex in our society is
being degraded into not merely an animal activity but even a
mechanical one, and that our sexuality is constantly being cor-
rupted by violence and greed, ours is also an age in which greater
openness in the discussion and practice of sexual activity has made
us less ignorant and fearful concerning it than any former generation in recent history. We can rejoice at the changes which have
enlightened our attitudes towards it, and dispelled many of the
appalling superstitions that used to surround it. While doing so,
it is all too easy to forget that a higher price is now being paid by
those for whom Christian morality as officially promoted (no
matter how liberally it may be phrased) still means a confrontation
with the word 'never'. For some, of course, it means never again,
as not all single people are in the position of 'not knowing what
they are missing' – which makes precious little difference anyway.

One can blame the permissive society for unhappy and exploitative sexual relationships, but it is absurd to blame it for the sexual
frustration experienced by some adult single people who have
never experienced intercourse, or who are faced with the possibility of never experiencing it again. A recent study[1] tells us that
even in enclosed convents some women do not find sexual
abstinence an easy matter, though insulated not only from men
but also from the mass media which are supposed to inflame our

passions (most of them are in fact aimed at inflaming the passions of men). Outside the convents it now seems to be taken for granted that Christian women who do not want to abstain will marry, and that any woman who has not adjusted to marriage or abstinence by her mid-twenties is either a huge joke or a case for the psychiatrist. Single women are affected by the temptations of the permissive society, but also and much more by their own *better* instincts, the desire to use their sexual capacities in a satisfying relationship with a real person, and by the huge volume of propaganda, both Christian and non-Christian, in favour of marriage and motherhood and of sexual activity as an ingredient of them.

I have seen Christians as well as non-Christians express both disgust and amusement when confronted by the sexual frustration of the single person; and in Christian teaching the whole question can still be swept quickly under the carpet in words such as these:

> People, whether married or single, who live for others and exercise their creativity in their work, art or other useful ways find that they are free from the demand for the physical aspects of sex.[2]

I am sure, however, that most Christians, if asked whether they really relished the idea of their daughter or son or sister or brother or friend never having any sexual relationships, would take this question as seriously as the threat of lifelong poverty or even physical handicap.

Christian writers on the single woman do take this problem seriously, and offer help in the personal aspects, such as dealing with the habit of masturbation or with feelings of envy and self-pity. But even those who are single by choice, or whose sexual drive is naturally low, are not exempt from the social penalties attached not only to being single but specifically to being permanently celibate. It is a social handicap quite comparable with illiteracy, and works in much the same way. One is cut off completely from an enormous area of human experience, and continually suspected of being lacking in normal human capacities, and this not only by the flibbertigibbets of the permissive society, but also by one's friends, family and professional counsellors. An adult mind condemned to live off the chewed-over remains of adolescent fantasy cries out for some real experience to feed on, and the woman who must inhabit the world of the single, where all sexual relationships take place outside the established moral code, is at a great disadvantage if she feels that she must preserve her virginity at all costs and so does not know where the real dangers lie. Even those who respect a single woman for her celibacy sometimes use her inexperience in this respect as an excuse for treating her as a non-adult in other respects as well, and though lack of sexual experience is not in itself a sign of an immature personality (it could well be the reverse), the more a woman is mature in other ways, the more her immaturity in this respect is likely to pain her.

The over-valuation of sexual experience in our society is connected – whether as cause or effect it is hard to say – with a great decline in other opportunities for physical and emotional intimacy. In the days when a single woman lived in a family home amid the seething loves and hatreds of about a dozen adults and children, she may have been able to use them to let off her own emotional steam. Similarly, our society used to be very much more hospitable towards intensely emotional (not necessarily sexual) friendships between women. Nowadays women are taught to expect their emotional satisfaction entirely from men. The stormy friendships and family life of the Victorians may seem to us unhealthy and rather ludicrous, but they could well have been better than nothing. To express love physically, other than in sexual relationships, is now socially suspect except with one's immediate family or very young children, and plenty of single women are isolated from even the most casual touch of another human being. Abstention from sexual relationships can mean total lack of physical and emotional contact with other people, something that even Jesus himself did not entirely forgo (John 13.23; Luke 7.38; John 21. 15–17). Sexual relationships outside marriage are dangerous, but it is a healthy instinct that tells us that playing with fire is better than freezing to death.

While not disputing that many women live happy and fulfilled lives in which sexual activity has no part, I find the theories by which Christians assert that any woman should and can do so if required, not convincing. The Christian teaching on celibacy is still derived from the days when to be a Christian celibate meant to live in a religious community. It was developed for those who had chosen to be celibate. This does not mean that they did not experience difficulties, but suitability for celibate life was and still is one of the requirements for admittance to such a community, and those who failed too conspicuously to maintain celibacy could be required to leave. I can find no evidence that celibacy experienced as permanently against one's will has ever been considered pleasing to God. Even Paul, who certainly favoured celibacy over marriage, was against involuntary celibacy (I Cor. 7.9), as was also the writer of I Timothy (5.14).

The traditional teaching looks forward to the kingdom of Heaven, where marriage will no longer exist and love will be universal. Many individuals and communities have tried to practise this universal love on earth, avoiding 'particular friendships' with other individuals. This tradition seems to have lost a good deal of its force today. Margaret Evening, for example, sees close friendship with one other person, of either sex, as a valuable foundation on which universal love can be built, such friendships becoming dangerous only if the friends become possessive, jealous or indifferent to other people.[3] This does not, surely, differ essentially from the teaching of Anne Townsend and others on the need for married people to use their mutual love as a foundation for wider relationships. The distinction between friendship and sexual partnership has become unimportant in this context.

The idea that sexual abstinence confers any kind of spiritual power is also on the decline. Though one can still find the hydraulic theory of sex by which its energy, if not expressed physically, can be channelled into love for others,[4] it appears that the majority of Christians have long since stopped thinking of love as being rationed like time and money, but rather as a capacity which increases with use, like intelligence. In recent controversies over the celibacy of the Roman Catholic clergy, the view has often been expressed that the celibate person is not suited to be the pastor of a predominantly married community, and even that celibacy is a disadvantage when helping other people in personal difficulty and temptation. This may well be untrue, but the growth of this opinion shows that the traditional virtues of the celibate state are going into eclipse, and have not so far been replaced by others. Traditional teaching has been much diluted, if not discredited.

For women, the picture is even more confusing as a result of the Christian teaching that non-celibacy means marriage, and the current assumption that all women would marry if they could. It is easy to get into a circular argument that women need marriage because they need sex because they need marriage and so on, and it reinforces the belief that women can only be hurt by intercourse outside a context of 'love' and 'permanence'. There is still a tendency to split the problem in half and assume that for men it is mainly physical and for women mainly emotional. Only among non-Christians, who are prepared to consider sex and marriage as different goals, can one find any serious consideration as to whether sexual activity is really essential for every woman's happiness – and it may surprise some Christians to learn that on the whole it is the 'Establishment' of psychology who think it is, and the radicals and feminists (Margaret Adams, for example) who think it is not.

The traditional view of female sexuality as being composed of the desire for children, a home and a life of caring for others, is extremely persistent, so much so that it is not easy to find words to describe its hidden side that is not bound up with domesticity or even with love for a particular man. Thielicke compares the sexual drive with the instinct for danger which makes men risk their lives in hazardous jobs and sports and war, a hunger for direct experience. This is a very masculine analogy, but (like men) some women desire intercourse as direct experience, and for this there can be no substitute. This desire is much stronger in some women than others, and stronger at different ages in the same woman, but while it is there it will not be dislodged even by a return to mediaeval scourging and starving. I am afraid that those who believe that sexual desire can be abolished by good works and creative activity will find that, on the contrary, any hard physical or mental effort tends to increase it; the penalty of coming to feel more alive is that one becomes more sensitive to frustration. What *is* true is that happiness and self-confidence generated by constructive activities compensate to some extent for unhappiness caused by this and other deprivations. They compensate but they do not substitute.

Probably only a minority of single women would name sexual frustration as the worst of their problems, but consideration of this subject shows very clearly how the traditional one-sided view of woman's nature can impose on the single woman a false view of herself. She is encouraged to accept her sexual frustration only if her sexual drives are focussed on marriage and motherhood. If this is not the case she is in danger of being tempted to pretend to herself that she is celibate by choice when this is not true, or to feel unnecessary guilt for having desires not 'natural' to women. The distinction between a natural desire for sexual experience as self-fulfilment, and a sinful desire to exploit other people for sexual pleasure, seems to be far more clearly appreciated when it is the nature of men that is being considered. Traditional teaching about women limits not only their actions but also their thoughts and feelings, and this can happen with other instincts also. The aggressive woman, for example, finds that most of the constructive uses of aggression are reserved for men and that women are supposed to be gentle and passive by nature. Freedom to know oneself is vital for emotional and spiritual growth, even when action has to be inhibited by considerations of morality and prudence, not to mention lack of opportunity.

17 | *The quality of life outside the family*

> People who have no-one to turn to for perspective, no
> helping resources in crises, no escape channels in difficulty,
> are impoverished indeed, though they live in conditions of
> plenty (R. & R. Rapoport, *Dual-career Families Re-examined*).[1]

The question of the sexual life of the single woman is itself a
complex issue, yet it also has an important bearing on two much
wider questions that are to take up the remainder of this book.
The first concerns the way in which single and married people live
as part of society as a whole: granted that single people do not
fit into it as well as married people, what sort of society is it, and
how could it be changed? The second question is: while the single
woman's condition arises, obviously, from the fact that she is single,
why does it make so much difference that she is also a woman?

The real or alleged sexual frustration of single people is often
included in the mental balance-sheet by which we compare the
married and the single states. Items from this balance-sheet appear
in all the literature of the subject, usually cited with the intention
of convincing both married and single people that the grass is not
greener on the other side of the fence. Other items might be the
loss of independence in marriage compared with the single person's vulnerability to loneliness, childlessness opposed to the end-
less anxieties of child-rearing, and so on. It is easy to show that
marriage entails one set of potential miseries and single life
another. The inclusion of sexual frustration on the list, however,
reminds us that nobody in their right mind expects life to be
entirely free from frustration and misery, but that most people
hope to find experiences of joy and comfort that will compensate
them for the dark days, and that most people (rightly or wrongly)
expect to find such experiences in their sexual lives.

When drawing up this mental balance-sheet, and considering
that vague set of circumstances known collectively as the 'quality
of life', it is therefore appropriate and even essential to include the
bonuses, the positively enjoyable experiences that are not necessary for survival, but compensate for the sorrows that come the

way of all but the most fortunate. That is why it is important to keep in mind the distinction between sexual frustration and loneliness. A chronically lonely person is in real danger of psychological deterioration, a sexually deprived person is not, but such people are not being unreasonable if they feel that they are *relatively* deprived, that they are as it were living on bread and water. Finally, consideration of sexual deprivation reminds us that for the single person all the positive experiences of their 'quality of life' must be sought outside the family.

The celebrated custom of wife-lending among the old-style Eskimo existed, so I understand, not only because they had a very liberal attitude to extra-marital affairs, but also because they had practically no other form of recreation available, and to sleep alone in the polar night was to risk death. Speaking metaphorically, we are not very far off the same situation. Our public emotional climate simply does not have enough warmth in it to sustain life in us, and our daily existence is so full of tension and stress that some form of intense release, physical or emotional and preferably both, is virtually necessary for us to remain truly human beings. I claim no originality for this statement, which has been used by others to account for increases in crime, drunkenness and drugtaking, and (in other ages) witchcraft, as well as sexual permissiveness. For the majority, however, this release of tension must take a more socially acceptable form, and the family is the socially acceptable context for sexual activity and for most other manifestations of the intimate, playful, creative and emotional side of the personality. People outside the family are like the canaries in the mine; they are the first to sense the dangerous deterioration in the social atmosphere. They are pitied as being deprived of family life, but their problems demonstrate that we are all, married and single alike, deprived of a satisfactory community life. Loneliness is endemic in our society; it is not a problem of single people alone, and remedying it is not their sole responsibility.

I think it is very significant that most of the solutions that are commonly suggested for relieving the loneliness of single women involve changing their private lives, by altering the way they live at home. A return to life in the 'extended family' (most single women I know regard this one with horror), or the founding of a community, or *ad hoc* plans for sharing a home with a friend or lover, may improve the quality of life for the individuals concerned, but perhaps such solutions are not sufficiently ambitious.

Many single women genuinely prefer to live alone, and would be quite content to go on doing so if only they could be more certain of getting help in times of crisis, and also of obtaining more companionship and satisfying activities outside their homes. Looking at the problem from this angle, however, involves turning away from the life of the individual single person and the possibility of reducing his or her degree of loneliness, and trying to do something about a society in which the danger of loneliness is a built-in feature.

At the risk of offending those married people who do contribute to the life of their communities, I am bound to say that it seems to me that most spare-time charity work, arts, sports, political and religious enterprises are in need of much more support from married people than they are currently getting, especially from younger married people and married men. The quality of leisure and community activities such as these has to be very high indeed if single people are to find in them anything like the satisfactions that married people expect from marriage, and if they are to go beyond being merely a palliative for loneliness to an attempt to attack it at the roots. Too many helpers of the single seem to feel that they have solved the problem if the single person can be fixed up with some kind of social outing once or twice a month. It helps, of course, and depending on what kind of meeting is involved, it can help a great deal and provide positively enjoyable experiences, but it is still expecting the single person to make do with a ration of community life which is only enough in fact for the married person, whose basic need for companionship is already being met within the family. Single people are also perhaps too ready to accept this situation, but they are now so few that they cannot be expected to change it without help from the married majority.

There is a frightening tendency in modern life for every human activity to be carried on either in a very small group in close intimacy, or in astronomical numbers in a mass, and very often both at the same time. Consider for example the passengers in a car, shut up together in their tin box yet isolated from everyone else on the road, or the diners in a restaurant trying to keep up their table's conversation above the noise of all the other conversations in the room. This may partly be the result of overpopulation in the absolute sense, but it also stems from the loss of a mid-dimension between the small unit and the crowd, and it is in this mid-dimension that single people should find their place. Some people, therefore, see the solution to the problems of single people in greater neighbourliness, in the revival of the small community where all the members know one another at least by name, feel able to call on one another at times of need, and join together in common celebrations. Many churches claim to be working towards the creation of such a community. They have a head start in this – again this is not an original idea – because they are one of the few social institutions left that cater for the whole person, not just as sportsmen or musicians or anarchists or whatever, and because the members already have common causes for celebration in their religious life, and common goals to work for in the service of God.

Single women may find, however, that building on the heritage of church and small-town community life may not work entirely to their advantage. The few single women I know who have lived in small rural communities where neighbourliness was a reality, tell me that they found that they could not do anything without the whole village getting to hear of it, and often reacting with disapproval. The Christian community has helped to preserve neighbourliness, but it has also helped to preserve some very conservative, not to say prejudiced, social attitudes, particularly concerning the role of women in society. Single people may well be reluctant to become part of a more closely-knit community if they feel that it is going to make them stand out more clearly as social deviants. They need a community based on new conventions of behaviour, not on a revival of traditional ones. If the Christians try to extend renewed community life to non-believers as well, as I think they certainly should, there will be even greater 'deviance' to be taken into account. Nor can the Christian community claim to cater for the whole person, in the case of single people, until it gives them more support in leading their sexual lives. Single people *are* in a sense deviants, and often have attitudes which differ greatly from the majority view not only towards sex but also in such matters as money, children and the future.

Being much alone, and particularly being alone in public, not only makes the single person more sensitive to the poverty of public life, but also more critical of the society that tolerates it. If I go to a formal party or reception, for example, I not only feel at a social disadvantage as half a couple, I also feel that we need a better way of introducing large numbers of people to one another than standing them in a stuffy and noisy room and filling them up with alcohol. If I travel alone, I become more conscious of the amenities of the places I visit, than I would if my attention were distracted by a companion. And of course a woman who habitually goes about without a man becomes very aware of the general lack of respect for women's needs and rights in our society. Being lonely has not only made me miserable, it has made me angry. As a single person, one becomes very critical of the defects of our society, not only as they affect single people, but in general. This makes me at the same time more and less pessimistic about the possibility of improving the single woman's condition. On the one hand it seems to make the chances of personal solutions to individual problems less likely, but on the other hand it offers a chance of lessening the sense of personal inadequacy, and of turning away from one's own selfish concerns towards new directions of purpose. Being single is an incentive to introspection, to examining one's own personality and its possible development, but it should be an incentive to looking outwards as well.

18 | *New directions*

> The men of grace have found
>   Glory begun below,
> Celestial fruits on earthly ground
>   From faith and hope may grow
>   (Isaac Watts).

In short, I am thoroughly fed up with discussions of the single person's state that consist entirely of delving around in our souls and characters to find out where *we* went wrong. I wish that those who are qualified to do so would devote some energy to more objective and practical study of ways to improve our social environment in general, and more specifically to remove the social disadvantages now suffered by single people. Perhaps some of the extra tax revenues collected from single people could be used to finance projects aimed at raising the quality of life outside the family.

The most urgent and obvious need is for serious and large-scale research into the experiences and attitudes of single people themselves, to find out what they consider to be the major issues of single life, and what improvement to it they themselves could suggest. Up to now far too many studies of single life have turned out to be studies of twenty or so divorced Americans, all under thirty-five and all in white-collar jobs. Journalists' pieces on single life have a tendency to concentrate too much on either the problems or the advantages of being single, with under-representation of what I believe to be the majority of single people, those who are sometimes glad to be single and sometimes not. What is most needed is not so much enquiry into how single people feel about single life, but enquiry into the factors in their social environments that have made them feel that way.

Using public money would also be desirable for my next priority, a study of matchmaking with the help of third parties. In view of what I said earlier about the problems caused for single people by attempts to marry them off, this may seem strange, but it must be acknowledged that some single people really believe they would be happier married, and that they may need help in finding a partner. Marriage as a right is now established as a social and legal concept. It appears in the UN Charter of Human Rights, and more generally it is considered very unacceptable for anyone, such as a parent for example, to prevent another person from marrying. (It is a pity that the right to single life is not so well established.) We ought to explore what the concept of a right to marriage means in terms of helping the unwillingly single person to find someone to marry. Most enterprises that claim to do this are extremely expensive, and some at least are strongly suspected of not giving good value for money. It will not help to abolish them, however, without putting something in their place, and for this some kind of public subsidy might be necessary. All single people would benefit if the number of unwillingly single people were reduced, since it would be easier to get a clear perspective on the needs of the single life considered in itself.

Another useful direction for thought would be the possibility of deliberate attempts to tip the balance of social status in favour of single people. What might happen, for instance, if parents transferred to some other day of celebration the money and attention now lavished on a daughter on her wedding day? I remember feeling justly proud of myself on the day when I landed my first job and was able to tell my father that I did not need any more of his money. It would have been nice to be able to share that feeling of achievement – his as well as mine – with more people. Christians could perhaps make more of changes in religious status, such as confirmation or adult baptism, but the fact is that in secular terms these ceremonies do not as a rule mark the achievement of adulthood. Perhaps some new ceremony should be introduced for those who have attained some turning-point in life, such as going to live away from home for the first time, or simply the age of legal majority. In such a ceremony I should like to see not only emphasis on the need for God's help in the future, but also thanksgiving for the past, with a clear indication that it *is* past, and that the person concerned, though unmarried, is no longer a child. (On second thoughts, this would be even more essential for those who have not left their parents' home.) Perhaps this ceremony could be supplemented later on by an equivalent of the silver and golden weddings. Not all single people could face such a celebration without embarrassment, but for some it would provide an opportunity to celebrate a happily single life and to share their happiness with the community, spreading the news that single life is not inevitably a problem or a 'nothing'.

Such ideas may sound a little frivolous when compared with considerations of real economic disadvantage, such as the difficulties of the single parent, or the single person caring for aged dependants, or the desperate shortage of reasonably-priced accommodation for single people. Some single people strongly resent the fact that they have to subsidize other people's families by taxation, rates, pension contributions and so on. Such resentments need sympathetic consideration, but also detailed study not possible here. Moreover, legal and economic change is unlikely ever to come about unless the general attitude to single life is altered, and ceremony and custom do greatly affect people's attitudes in such matters, not least the attitudes of single people towards each other.

As I said in the previous chapter, however, single people have the right to criticize their society not only as it affects them, but as it affects all its members. This means that the range of possible action for change that can be undertaken by Christian single people is not limited to direct intervention in single life. Single people will be the first, but not the only, people to benefit from any enterprise that makes the world of work more humanly satisfying or extends the boundaries of friendliness and interdependence outside the emotional boundaries of the nuclear family.

Of course it will not be possible to reach agreement in detail about what constitutes an ideal society, but there might well be some consensus among single people about general aims. We need to move away from the idea that people work only for money, not only money to live on but also as an indicator of social status, and that they will do anything at any time in order to earn more, towards the idea that people also need to feel that their work is useful, towards individual pride and satisfaction with what they do, and towards the sensible integration of work with the rest of life (by working flexible hours, for example). Single people might also feel committed to support any enterprise that provided cheap high-quality public facilities (such as transport), instead of private facilities for those who can afford them, thus conserving resources and providing greater opportunities for neighbourliness. They would welcome better public care for the aged and the sick, since private care is unlikely to come their way. Single people benefit from any enterprise that fosters co-operation rather than competition, inter-dependence rather than dependence, participation rather than being a spectator. If anyone is beginning to suspect political overtones here, they are quite right, but I am only putting forward very general principles, not advocating acceptance of any of the political philosophies now on the market.

There is nothing specifically Christian about change of this kind; indeed such enterprises provide good opportunities for Christians to work alongside others. I am not one of those Christians who think that when one is financially secure and physically healthy one should ask no more of this world, nor do I think that loneliness in our society is insignificant when compared to the poverty and disease and other forms of suffering which are so prevalent in other parts of the world. Just as the poverty and disease of many countries will never be effectively relieved without fairly drastic social and political changes, so it is unlikely that much can be done about loneliness in our society without at the least some forceful criticism of society as it is now.

I quite realize that action along these lines is not going to change the life of any individual single person overnight, or perhaps ever. I do believe it is important, however, that single people should at least realize that they are not quite so helpless in face of their condition as they may think. As Christians they should already know something about unselfish service and co-operation, to be exercised not only among family but also among neighbours, and as single people they are likely to have had personal experience of loneliness and social disadvantage, which makes them able to sympathize with others in the same situation. Best of all, they know when intervention has to stop, they know the value of solitude and independence. Finding oneself a social misfit is very educational, and surely *some* good must come of knowing more about the way society works. Perhaps these insights are to be expected in middle age, perhaps married people too come to perceive some of them. Amateurish as my analysis of society may be, however, I have a strong feeling that if I had married I could have lived to be a hundred without any of these ideas ever occurring to me.

Similarly, one can expect that many single people, having thought the matter over, will simply continue with their recreations and their voluntary work, and their personal relationships, exactly as before. For some, however, even a change of attitude could be all-important. It may sound a little high-flown and old-fashioned to call single people the forerunners on earth of the universal love to be expected in the kingdom of Heaven, and single people will vary in what they think they can or ought to do to practise this love, but at least it is certainly healthier to think of oneself as the forerunner of a better society than as the outcast of the present one.

In this context a slightly more militant attitude on the part of single people would, I think, be helpful. They could be just a little bit more ready to stand up for their way of life, to protest against disparaging remarks about single life and single individuals, and to assert the rights of friendship and neighbourliness against the rights of marriage and the family. They could be more ready to talk openly about the advantages and disadvantages of single life, not only with one another but also with the married majority.

To change attitudes, however, one must first be confirmed in one's own beliefs. It is here that one reaches the root of the problems of the single woman, as distinct from those of the single person in general. Other writers have treated the problems of the single woman as being basically a crisis of self-confidence, but they see the remedy entirely in personal terms. They provide advice, much of it excellent, on developing talent and character, by shaking off apathy and seeking a more purposeful way of life. They urge the single woman to look to God for strength and consolation, and for a new self-confidence based on her relationship to him:

> You are a jewel of infinite value to be set as a blazing ornament for the King of Kings.[1]

One might think this would be enough, but it is not. Restoring the self-confidence of the single woman demands as part of her religion some answer to the question of what women are for. It is doubt and confusion about her womanhood that drains away the self-confidence of the single woman, not just deprivation of the benefits of marriage, or the obvious disadvantages of being alone in a marriage-based society. True loneliness is the feeling that one has nothing to offer other people, and being single generates this feeling in women (just as being unemployed often seems to generate it in men). It is caused not so much by the disadvantages of her status, as by her acceptance of the culture on which these disadvantages are based, and which justifies their existence. I think this accounts for the fact that so many single women who do not wish to marry, are materially well off, and do not lack for companionship, are still often quite unaware of the advantages of their situation or unable to think coherently about it at all. If the single woman can do nothing else to improve her lot, she can still benefit enormously by a spell of prolonged hard thought about what she has been told about the nature and social role of women, and by testing it against the reality of her own experiences and feelings, and those of other women.

19 | *What are women for?*

> I deny that anyone knows, or can know, the nature of the
> two sexes, as long as they have only been seen in their
> present relation to one another (J. S. Mill, *On the
> Subjection of Women*, 1869).

The study and criticism of traditional opinions on sexual morality
has had wider uses beyond helping me to reach certain conclusions
on that particular issue. It also provides clear statements of ideology on the subject of women's nature which in other aspects of
life, such as employment and family relationships, is not taught so
explicitly but spread by example and social conditioning. Thielicke,
for example, demonstrates how misconceptions about the sexual
nature of women are just part of a larger misconception about
their nature as a whole:

> The woman is identified with her sexuality quite differently from
> the man. It is, so to speak, the 'vocation' of the woman to be
> lover, companion and mother. And even the unmarried woman
> fulfils her calling in accord with the essential image of herself
> only when these fundamental characteristics, which are designed
> for wifehood and motherhood, undergo a sublimating trans-
> formation, but still remain discernible . . .[1]

If this were true, one could not deny that the single woman who
is not leading a dedicated life defined within fairly narrow limits
is a failure. There is no room for anyone but the saintly maiden
and the godly matron. Even so, the single woman is placed in a
second-class position in that, with the spiritual life of woman
based entirely on biology, she cannot express her vocation directly
in an actual relationship with a man.

This is the majority view. If you ask: 'What are human beings
for?' there is an infinite number of possible answers, some much
more profound than others, and many that contradict one another.
If you ask: 'What are men for?' the range of answers is only
slightly narrower. But if you ask: 'What are women for?' everyone
knows the answer, and whether expressed in four-letter words or

texts from the Bible it is still the same answer: that it is not good for *man* to live alone. It is the same answer from those who serve God and those who do not, and this alone ought to make us suspect that it might be the wrong answer. When it comes down to how women actually spend their time, it matters little whether they and their menfolk worship God or the devil, women still end up living *for men*.

Living for men obviously means that most women have husbands and children, and derive most of their social status and sense of achievement from these relationships. It also means, however, that all women live in a society where most of the important decisions in their lives are made for them by men. When they appear to have a choice, it is between alternatives that men have provided. Single women have more control than wives over their own time, talents and money, but they are only relatively more autonomous; they too live in a society where power is masculine. Even the enclosed nun has vowed obedience to a hierarchy whose upper ranks are all men. The stereotyping of the single woman as either nun or whore derives from the stereotyping of all women as either Eve or Mary, instruments of man's ruin or his salvation. If single women are frustrated in their work, all women's work is less rewarding in terms of choice of employment, pay and creative opportunity. Efforts to enjoy leisure and make new friends are restricted by the conventions that govern women's public behaviour, in a society in which woman's place is in the home. If single women court disaster in sexual relationships, it is because women's sexual rights are not recognized except in marriage, and there only by limiting them to a single relationship. Whenever women gain access to some new privilege, there is always a long debate as to whether they should be allowed (by men) to have it, and whether it will distract them from their duties as wives and mothers. Though the vocation of women to live for men is supposed to stem from instinct, in fact a good deal of social conditioning is needed to make them accept it; and if it is true that God commanded men to rule over women, it is strange how many men obey this commandment who would never think of obeying any other.

Sooner or later there comes a day in the life of any woman, married or single, when some incident, possibly quite trivial, makes her realize that she is being pushed around, not because she is really in the wrong, or really stubborn or stupid, but because she is a woman. Sometimes she gets her own way in the end by strategy, but in a clash of wills she is more often forced to submit, because men hold most positions of authority, and have an overwhelmingly greater share of the power derived from money, education, and technical and political know-how. When self-esteem, common sense and conscience are repeatedly overborne by the will of others, it becomes hard to keep them alive, and women do indeed often sacrifice them to adapt to their subordinate social role. Our society is run according to man's view of women, which is surprisingly often, especially in the case of single women, quite different from women's view of themselves. Their situation can be compared to that of African or Oriental civilizations under European colonial rule.

The single man, however wretched in his personal life, is at least free to discover his own reasons for finding life worth living, and his own ways of serving God. The 'essential image' of man is not limited to being lover, companion and father. As Thielicke says, woman is 'identified with her sexuality quite differently from the man', because she has been totally identified with it. Everything she is and does, she must do and be as a woman, not as a human being. Living in a subordinate social group thus distorts women's knowledge of themselves and limits their purposes in life, that is, it perverts their religion.

Both in and outside the Christian community, women are taught to believe that they can best please God by pleasing man, and by accepting the role of his subordinate, comforter, homemaker and dispenser of happiness, who does all the little routine jobs that keep life going for him. The gospel, however, teaches that it is the duty of all Christians to minister to others, and their privilege too, and one cannot get round this by saying that because one sex (men) tends to find some forms of ministry more of a duty than a privilege, the other sex (women) can be called upon to perform them as their privilege 'by nature'. Women are naturally just as lazy and selfish as men. Forcing them into altruistic behaviour by limiting their choices of action does not really help to make them better Christians. Women can hear God's commandments for themselves, and decide for themselves how they will obey them; there is no need to shout in one ear that it is woman's 'nature' to serve God by living for men, and in the other ear that single women must be sure to live for men likewise, though debarred from doing so in the 'natural' way. The rule of men over women is not necessarily always tyrannical, but it is wrong all the same, because it has become an usurpation of God's authority.

Thielicke's essential image of woman is just that, an image invented by men. If women are ever to find out what the reality of their nature is, they must question all traditional images and think of themselves as human beings first – with all that this implies both now and in the future – and women second. There is nothing very new in this as a theoretical teaching: 'There is no such thing as Jew or Greek, slave and freeman, male and female, for you are all one person in Jesus Christ' (Gal. 3.28). Christians have gradually come to realize that our status as human beings means that it is wrong for the rich to control the lives of the poor, and wrong for one race to control the lives of another. If this text means anything, it also means that women are the children of God on equal terms with men. With humanity and being the child of God comes the Spirit which is 'poured out upon *all* flesh' (Joel 2.28), and this means that women must not deny their own consciousness even when it is in conflict with the consciousness of men. There have, of course, always been women who have lived in this way, who have done great things in spite of constant hindrances from the very people who would have been the first to help them if they had been men. Weaker sisters, however, could also contribute to God's work, if they were freed from social and mental constraints based on a false view of woman's nature.

Other writers on the Christian single woman have perceived that men have social dominance over women, but they attach little importance to the fact, and give superficial and contradictory answers to the very fundamental question of why this should be so:

> The heart of every true woman centers around her relationship to men, and rightfully so. It's the way God created us.[2]

> I'm wondering if this immense, clinging, psychological dependence on man which is part of us as women is not something we should face as part of our fallenness.[3]

Miss Sands devotes a whole chapter to reasserting the ideal of the single woman as a heroine in her work but a lady in her demeanour, accepting men's authority even when she realizes they are less capable than herself. Gini Andrews, very shrewdly, points out that the Bible demands only submission of wife to husband, and deplores the behaviour of some single men who demand cherishing by single women to which only a husband has a right. She does not realize, however, that the dependence that keeps some women washing their boy friends' shirts and listening to their complaints without much reward is social as well as psychological. Men sometimes become psychologically dependent on women, but they do not as a rule get the idea that they must be submissive to all women if they hope to find a wife some day.

A large part of *Your half of the apple* is devoted to self-improvement, and the author emphasizes that this is desirable whether marriage eventually takes place or not:

> Most of the things a single girl can be doing to make herself attractive and intriguing to the opposite sex are things which develop and expand her as a whole woman.

In all aspects of this development, however, the ultimate aim is that of becoming a strong candidate for marriage:

> Are you developing the brain God gave *you* so that your man will find you stimulating and interesting?

This explicitly means that development cannot be unlimited:

> Are you *over*-developing the brain God gave you so that you're becoming Miss Know-it-all and a bore? With some notable exceptions I'm convinced that there aren't many things more upsetting to the male ego than the female super-brain.[4]

There really is an intellectual discrepancy between believing that the dependence of woman on man is not God's will, and yet believing that all women need to be dependent on one man in marriage, between urging women to become all that God has made it possible for them to become, yet stopping them short if it alienates them from man. And once one admits that there could be a difference between man's 'whole woman' and God's, one is forced to make a choice between them as the goal of self-development.

These writers have not neglected to state the practical implications of their beliefs about what women are for, and those who hold other beliefs must be prepared to face the practical implications too. Few writers, even feminists, seem aware of the extent to which singleness, in our society, is used as the ultimate deterrent against women, both married and single. In practice if not in theory, most men do expect submissive behaviour from all women, not only from their wives, and are often in a position to enforce it. Any woman who objects is very likely to be told, more or less explicitly, that she risks becoming the kind of woman who cannot get a man, or will lose the man she does have, and will be obliged to face life on her own. I have tried to show that the disadvantages of single life are by no means all imaginary, and that they are worse for women because single women are seen as having 'failed' to please men, or as having 'rebelled' against nature and the social order. I believe therefore that in the long run there are no personal solutions to the problems of the single woman. The only effective change will be a change in the social status of women as a whole. Single men are sometimes credited as a social class as being more likely than husbands to go in for crime or political agitation, but this is a minor threat to the *status quo* compared with the threat posed by the happily independent woman. It is not in the interests of the social structure to make single life attractive to women, and so all its disadvantages tend to get perpetuated.

> Real love is effective. If you really love you do something
> about it, and do it as well as you can manage to learn how
> . . . Perhaps the most successful anti-love device of our
> clever culture has been this separation of love from
> technique . . . if we once learned to link love and technique
> our culture would come apart at the seams (Rosemary
> Haughton, *Love*).

The idea that women should live for men is based on two premises, which though closely connected can be considered separately. Both are found in Christian and non-Christian ideology. The first is that men and women are endowed with different but complementary qualities, so that human nature at its best is seen only when the two are together in partnership. The second is that power should be attached to the 'masculine' qualities, and therefore to men. The latter idea is the practical reason why the single woman, though not directly under the control of one man, still finds it so difficult to control her own life. There are other much more serious consequences. It is even possible that the inequality of power between the sexes may some day destroy the human race, because the so-called 'feminine' values of patience, humility, loyalty and compassion, which are so highly rated in Christianity (and in most other religions too), have been rendered socially powerless by being relegated to women and so to private life. They are not being used to counterbalance the equally essential 'masculine' values of courage, objectivity, order, the urge to explore and dominate the environment and to discover new ideas, that control our public and political life. Men and women have gone into partnership not to learn each other's virtues but to have someone else be virtuous on their behalf. (One can see the same thing happening on a small scale in some marriages.) Christian feminists have already stated the need for the partnership of man and woman to be more equal, and hence more effective, but I think that the single woman needs to study the concept of partnership in more detail and apply it to individual relationships as well as to man and woman in general.

The old ideals of dedicated celibacy, however unattractive they may seem to us today, did at least allow Christian women other purposes in life besides marriage and motherhood, and admitted that partnership between men and women could take other forms than marriage. Single women today are forced to confront the fact that partnership between man and woman is now understood as the global partnership between the two halves of the human race, or partnership of two individuals in marriage. The lack of any intermediate or alternative form has coloured Christian as well as non-Christian thinking, and some Christians have, it seems, adopted the basically unchristian view that the single woman is only half a human being:

> You are in some ways incomplete until you have found completion with the right man: not just sexual completion but marriage.[1]

It is not a very long step from this to the old stereotypes of the single person as abnormal, and to the non-Christian devaluation of virginity.

Other writers on the Christian single woman have questioned this idea of incompleteness of the single woman, but not by opposing it directly; they approach it by way of considering the relationship between the single woman and God:

> God didn't *just* design us to be wives and mothers . . . we are made in the image of God with a spirit as well as an animal body.[2]

Yes, but just as being a wife and mother involves more than the animal body, being a single woman involves more than the spirit. Margaret Evening also takes this approach to the ideal of human nature:

> Man may be called to fulfil God's purposes for him through bypassing or transcending in some way the man-woman polarity, or at least by dissociating it from the purely biological male-female relationship.[3]

I am not sure that a purely biological relationship can exist in human beings, and it is certainly not what Christians understand by marriage. Both these writers see the transcending of single life as a process of raising oneself above the natural level, where sexuality is so important, to a higher, 'spiritual' level. Would this process not be greatly assisted if women were allowed to recognize the *natural* side of their personalities that is not designed for marriage either? No one expects a marriage to come to full spiritual stature overnight. The spiritual aspect of marriage rests on a solid foundation of shared physical and domestic experience, and is built up not only by the individual partners but also by the community they live in. Similarly, the spiritual life of single people can only develop if it is integrated with the rest of their earthly lives and their membership of their community.

One possible way for Christians to build their lives on a partnership between 'masculine' and 'feminine' human nature is for them to try to achieve some completeness of human nature within themselves as individuals, building on the fact, which Margaret Evening also mentions, that all human beings possess to some degree qualities of both 'masculine' and 'feminine'. This process, however, runs counter to much of our early social conditioning. If the development of good qualities in every individual were no longer limited by assigning them to either men or women, some think that the result would be a race of freaks. Others think that there is a danger of producing androgynous beings living in sterile isolation with no emotional needs for anyone but themselves. One could argue, however, that the real differences between the sexes, those that God created, could not in fact be destroyed by any changes we might try to make, and that a society without sexual stereotypes would be more interesting than one in which women are encouraged to be boringly alike, and men can be as boringly alike as they wish provided they are not like women. For single people life might well be more satisfying if they could make more use of the other-sex side of their natures, and this would be true at all levels, not only the spiritual. To learn the virtues of the other sex one must first learn something of their practical and psychological skills. For example, a woman trying to become braver and more self-assertive would have to learn to keep cool in difficult situations and control her temper. A man trying to be more compassionate would have to learn the typically feminine art of observing other people for signs of hidden emotion. Ideally this process would begin in childhood, not in the third or fourth decade of life when singleness becomes one's destiny. This would involve considerable changes in our social climate.

Some social change will certainly be necessary if we are to create more opportunities for the expression of complete human nature in groups, teams and communities where one sex is in a minority or even absent altogether. At present, society lends support to only one form of man-woman partnership: marriage. In all other enterprises where both sexes work together, stereotyping tends to force men and women into behaviour that imitates the social roles of marriage, where these may be totally inappropriate. It also often results in the members of one sex (usually the women) doing all the work, and the other sex getting all the credit for the results.

The recognition of women as fully human beings, and the working out of this recognition in social terms, must therefore also involve questioning the traditional division of human nature into 'masculine' and 'feminine' natures. The traditionally 'feminine' virtues that are cultivated in women must receive a more equal share of power, but it must not be forgotten that they can be cultivated in men as well, and that some women possess a large share of the traditionally 'masculine' virtues. Unless this fact is kept in view when efforts are made to change the social structure, I think that the doubts and fears of some single women about themselves will not be laid to rest. It would be all too easy to create a new stereotype of womanhood to replace the old one. Though some people fear that the new ideal of womanhood is the Amazon, the virago (which already approximates to one of the negative stereotypes of the single woman), it could just as easily be another reincarnation of the Mother Goddess, the exaltation of fertility and increase. The True Woman must be buried once and for all, so that every woman can be free to discover what womanhood is for her as an individual. The complementary human qualities will remain, but their partnership must take on a much wider variety of forms.

This process, known rather inaccurately as 'women's liberation' (since in some ways it will liberate men as well) will not happen overnight and not all its effects are predictable. Speaking from my own experience, however, I can outline three likely results that can be looked for in the life of a single woman who comes to recognize the social and ideological factors in the condition of women in general.

Firstly, beginning to think of women as human beings and not primarily as the complements of men breaks down the barriers which isolate women from one another, and causes them to discover new and interesting characters behind familiar faces. Real liking, friendship and love become possible when other women are seen as more than rivals or allies in the struggle to get and hold the attention of men. Single and married women discover how much they have in common, stop looking at each other with mutual scorn or envy, and learn that their personal failures are in part the product of a social system. They can begin to hope and work for a collective as well as a personal improvement in their lives.

It also becomes more possible to achieve a Christian attitude towards men. It is commonly assumed that feminist women have rejected men, but this is true only of a small minority (often as a result of years of personal ill-treatment). Most women, whether feminist or not, harbour some hidden resentments against men, and to bring these into the open is a long step in the direction of overcoming them. To hate men or to become indifferent to them is obviously not a Christian solution, and it is not a truly feminist solution either. Liberation does not mean substituting automatic rebellion for automatic submission, and sisterhood is not founded only on an alliance to resist male oppression. Liberation means choice. By remembering that she must decide for herself whether co-operation or protest is appropriate to the occasion, a woman becomes more able to criticize men's behaviour, but also more able to appreciate it. It is easier to accept single life when one can see that men are not the answer to all one's needs, and relationships with them are more secure when one understands that they too are conditioned by social stereotyping. One values more highly the good qualities of men who in spite of this conditioning have learned some truth about women and about the 'feminine' side of their own natures. Not feeling obliged to be invariably compliant lessens the temptation to sudden outbreaks of bitchiness, and one is much better able to put one's energies into pleasing one man for his own sake, when one has given up trying to please all men just because they are men.

There may also, perhaps, be a change in our perception of God. Since we believe that he is all-powerful, we are at present obliged to think of him in terms of masculinity: Father, Lord, King, Judge. It has become next door to impossible to think of God as in any way female, because our view of female nature is so distorted and false. If humankind is made in God's image, the best qualities of woman must be his too, and we must try to find out what these qualities are, and bring them into our own lives. Trying to become more like God will no longer mean trying to become more masculine, or putting ourselves into relationships with him that are too similar to our earthly relationships with men, or trying to ignore our womanhood altogether and be altogether 'spiritual'. Liberating ourselves as women could mean that we help to liberate God too, bringing a little closer the day when all that is best in human nature can work together. If this happens, if power and compassion flourish together in both men and women as individuals, and in both halves of the entire human race, then indeed our self-destructive culture will collapse and anything is possible, even the coming of God's kingdom on earth.

Notes

Chapter 2 Upbringing

1. J. P. White, *Towards a Compulsory Curriculum*, Routledge & Kegan Paul 1973.
2. L. Cole and I. N. Hall, *Psychology of Adolescence*, 7th edn, Holt, Rinehart Winston 1970, pp. 639–648.
3. See A. Storr, *Human Aggression*, Penguin 1971.
4. Jacky Gillott, *For Better, for Worse: Marriage Today*, Penguin 1971.
5. See *Britain's Sixteen-year-olds* ed. K. R. Fogelman, National Children's Bureau 1976.
6. *Fifth Form Girls: Their Hopes for the Future* (Population Censuses and Surveys Office), HMSO 1975.
7. Eddie Neale, *We're All Afraid*, Scripture Union 1972.

Chapter 3 Vocations

1. F. Morley, *The Call of God*, SPCK 1959, p. 36.
2. Mary McCarthy, *Memories of a Catholic Girlhood*, Heinemann 1957.
3. K. W. Britton, *Philosophy and the Meaning of Life*, CUP 1969, p. 35.
4. Anglican nun, quoted by Geoffrey Moorhouse in *Against All Reason*, Weidenfeld & Nicolson 1969; Penguin 1972, pp. 205f.

Chapter 4 Choices

1. Branse Burbridge, *The Sex Thing*, Hodder 1972, p. 37.
2. Gini Andrews, *Your Half of the Apple*, Lakeland 1973, pp. 55f.
3. Jessie Bernard, *Academic Women*, Pennsylvania State University Press 1964.
4. See Claire Rayner, 'On the 25-plus shelf', *New Society*, 13 December 1973, pp. 654f.

Chapter 5 Work

1. I. Hilton, 'The decision to return' in *Women at Work* ed. B. Musgrave and J. Wheeler-Bennett, Peter Owen 1972, p. 15.
2. Claire Rayner, *The Shy Person's Book*, Wolfe Publishing 1973; Sara Delamont, *Interaction in the Classroom*, Methuen 1976.

Chapter 7 Family relationships

1. Janice Glover, *Sense and Sensibility for Single Women*, Doubleday 1963, ch. 15.

Chapter 8   Friends

1. Olive Johnson, *Living Alone*, New Zealand 1976, p. 52.
2. Audrey Lee Sands, *Single and Satisfied*, Tyndale House 1971, p. 28.

Chapter 9   The family of God

1. Rosemary Haughton, *Love*, C. A. Watts 1970; Penguin 1974, p. 133.
2. F. R. Barry, *Christian Ethics and the Secular Society*, Hodder 1966, p. 186.
3. Werner and Lotte Pelz, *God is no More*, Gollancz 1963; Penguin 1968, p. 37.
4. Anglican Commission, *Marriage, Divorce and the Church*, SPCK 1972, pp. 41f.

Chapter 10   The family of the church

1. Rosemary Haughton, *The Knife Edge of Experience*, Darton, Longman and Todd 1972, p. 110.

Chapter 11   Loneliness

1. See, for instance, Phyllis Chesler, *Women and Madness*, Allen Lane, 1974, and Jessie Bernard, *The Future of Marriage*, Souvenir Press 1973.
2. W. L. Carrington, *Psychology, Religion and Human Need*, Epworth Press 1956, p. 219.

Chapter 12   Sexual relationships: moral aspects

1. Stevie Smith, *Collected Poems*, Allen Lane, 1975, p. 167.
2. E. R. Matthews, *Sex, Love and Society*, Gollancz 1959, pp. 162f.
3. F. R. Barry, *Christian Ethics and the Secular Society*, p. 173.
4. Angela Carter, *Several Perceptions*, Heinemann 1968; Pan 1970, p. 98.

Chapter 13   The way forward: extending the moral frontier

1. Michael Keeling, *What is Right?*, SCM Press 1969.
2. Gini Andrews, *Your Half of the Apple*, p. 82.

Chapter 14   Sexual relationships: theological aspects

1. *Marriage, Divorce and the Church*, p. 17.
2. Joy Davidman, *Smoke on the Mountain*, Hodder 1955, p. 78.
3. Gini Andrews, *Your Half of the Apple*, p. 53.

Chapter 15   The way forward: a new theology

1. *Towards a Quaker View of Sex* ed. A. Heron, Friends Home Service Committee 1964.
2. Helmut Thielicke, *The Ethics of Sex*, James Clarke 1964, p. 201.
3. See Margaret Adams, *Single Blessedness*, Heinemann 1976.

Chapter 16   Celibacy

1. Marcelle Bernstein, *Nuns*, Lippincott, Philadelphia 1976.
2. E. Claxton and J. Fry, *Tomorrow's Parents*, Grosvenor Books 1977.
3. See also the Jesuit writer Donald Goergen, *The Sexual Celibate*, SPCK 1976.
4. In V. A. Demant's *Christian Sex Ethics: An Exposition*, Hodder 1963, for example.

Chapter 17   The quality of life

1. Rhona and Robert Rapoport, *Dual-career Families Re-examined*, Martin Robertson 1976.

Chapter 18   New directions

1. Gini Andrews, *Your Half of the Apple*, p. 31.

Chapter 19   What are women for?

1. Helmut Thielicke, *The Ethics of Sex*, p. 81.
2. Audrey Lee Sands, *Single and Satisfied*, p. 21.
3. Gini Andrews, *Your Half of the Apple*, p. 49.
4. Ibid., pp. 61, 39.

Chapter 20   Partnership

1. From an optional series of lessons 'On the Christian View of Sex and Marriage' offered in a girls' school; appendix A in Harold Loukes, *Teenage Religion*, SCM Press 1961.
2. Shelagh Brown, *Single*, Falcon 1971, p. 6.
3. Margaret Evening, *Who Walk Alone*, p. 128.

Bibliography

1. Books dealing wholly or partly with the subject of single women from a traditional point of view. All the authors are Christian but the amount of specifically Christian teaching varies widely.

Andrews, Gini, *Your Half of the Apple: God and the Single Girl*, Lakeland 1973.

Brown, Shelagh, *Single: Fulfilment and the Single Christian Woman*, Falcon Booklets 1971.

Burbridge, Branse, *The Sex Thing* (see esp. ch 4, 'On the Shelf'), Hodder 1972.

Clarkson, Margaret, *Single*, Kingsway Publications 1980.

Evening, Margaret, *Who Walk Alone: A Consideration of the Single Life*, Hodder 1974.

Glover, Janice, *Sense and Sensibility for Single Women*, Doubleday 1963.

Johnson, Olive, *Living Alone*, 1976. Published by the author and distributed by Price Milburn, Wellington, New Zealand.

Johnson, Paul E., *Pastoral Ministration*, James Nisbet 1955.

Laurence, J., *The Single Woman*, Duell, Sloan & Peach 1952.

Sands, Audrey Lee, *Single and Satisfied*, Tyndale House 1971.

Smith, Joyce Marie, *Fulfillment: Bible Studies for Women*, Tyndale House 1975.

Stephenson, Elspeth, *Enjoying Being Single*, Lion Publishing 1981.

Tigwell, John, 'The family in the church: to support and to care' in *Families, Facts and Frictions*, compiled by J. Tigwell, Scripture Union 1976.

Townsend, Anne, *Families without Pretending*, Scripture Union 1976.

2. Recommended for further reading.

a) A non-Christian, non-traditional point of view:

Adams, Margaret, *Single Blessedness: Observations on the Single Status in Married Society*, Heinemann 1976.

b) Two short American essays from the Christian feminist point of view on the single woman as church member:

Bequaert, Lucia H., *Single Women: Alone and Together* (ch 10, 'Women Alone in the Sight of God'), Beacon Press, Boston 1977.

Johnson, Kathy Jan, 'Single and Whole' in *Women in a Strange Land: Search for a New Image* edited by C. B. Fischer, B. Brenneman and A. M. Bennett, Fortress Press, Philadelphia 1975.

c) More general works:

Adams, C., and Laurikietis, R., *The Gender Trap: A Closer Look at Sex Roles*: Book 2, *Sex and Marriage*, Virago 1976.

Bennis, W. G., and Slater, P. E., *The Temporary Society*, Harper & Row 1968.

Bowskill, D., *People Need People*, Wildwood House 1977.

Brain, R., *Friends and Lovers*, Hart-Davis 1976.

Busfield, J., and Paddon, M., *Thinking About Children*, CUP 1977.

Cunneen, S., *Sex – Female; Religion – Catholic*, Burns & Oates 1969.

Gorman, C., *People Together: A Guide to Communal Living*, Paladin 1975.

Gray, C., 'Behaving according to plan', *Where?*, No. 126, March 1977, pp. 69–71. (A useful presentation of the socialization of girls.)

Greengross, W., *Entitled to Love: Sexual and Emotional Needs of the Handicapped*, National Marriage Guidance Council 1976.

Groombridge, J., *His and Hers: An Examination of Masculinity and Femininity*, Penguin 1971.

Hennig, M., and Jardim, A., *The Managerial Woman*, Marion Boyars 1978.

Hoffman, M. M., 'Assumptions in sex education books', *Educational Review*, Vol. 27, No. 3, June 1975, pp. 211–20.

Janeway, Elizabeth, *Man's World, Woman's Place*, Michael Joseph 1972.

King, J. S., *Women and Work: Sex Differences and Society*, HMSO 1974.

Kroll, Una, *Flesh of My Flesh*, Darton, Longman & Todd 1975.

Webb, Pauline, *Where are the Women?*, Epworth Press 1979.

Whitworth, J. M., *God's Blueprints: A Sociological Study of Three Utopian Sects*, Routledge 1975. (For the history of the Shakers.)

Williams, H. A., *Poverty, Chastity and Obedience: The True Virtues*, Mitchell Beazley 1975.